Trouble River

and Related Readings

McDougal Littell
A HOUGHTON MIFFLIN COMPANY
Evanston, Illinois • Boston • Dallas

Acknowledgments

Viking Penguin: *Trouble River* by Betsy Byars. Copyright © 1969 by Betsy Byars. Reprinted by arrangement with Viking Penguin, a division of Penguin Books USA, Inc.

Lerner Publications Company: Excerpt from *Buffalo Gals: Women of the Old West* by Brandon Marie Miller. Copyright © 1995 by Lerner Publications Company. All rights reserved. Used by permission of the publisher.

HarperCollins Publishers, Inc.: Excerpt from *On the Way Home* by Laura Ingalls Wilder. Copyright © 1962 by Roger Lea MacBride.

Music and lyrics for "Oh, Susanna," "Paddle Your Own Canoe," and "Buffalo Gals," from *The Laura Ingalls Wilder Songbook*, compiled and edited by Eugenia Garson. Original text copyright © 1968 by Eugenia Garson. Musical arrangements copyright © 1968 by Herbert Haufrecht. Used by permission of HarperCollins Publishers, Inc.

Golden Books Publishing Company, Inc.: "Old Sly Eye" by Russell Gordon Carter, from *Story Parade*. Copyright © 1945 by Story Parade, renewed in 1973. Used by permission of Golden Books Publishing Company, Inc.

Continued on page 134

Cover illustration by Lee Christiansen.
Background photograph Copyright © PhotoDisc.
Author image by Bashnan Studios.

Printed in the United States of America.

ISBN 0-395-77526-4

1234567—DCI—03 02 01 00 99 98 97

Contents

Trouble River

Betsy Byars

Contents

Chapter 1

An Uneasy Feeling

The woman sat in the door of the cabin rocking in her chair. With the hem of her apron she fanned herself, saying over and over, "Where is that boy? Where is that boy?"

She rose and moved to the open doorway where she looked out over the golden prairie.

"Dewey!" she called, her voice breaking with anxiety. *"Deweeeeeee."*

When there was no answer, she went back to her rocking chair.

"Dewey Martin," she called from her chair. "Oh, *Deweeee.*"

After a moment she went to stand in the doorway again. For as far as she could see there was only the prairie, the long waving line of grass on the horizon with not one single cabin or chimney in sight.

The sun was dropping behind the horizon, and she knew how quickly darkness would cover the land, how quickly the colorful prairie would become desolate and cold. The lines between her brows deepened.

"Well, I reckon I'll just have to go find him," she said to herself.

Holding her walking cane and the side of the door for support, she stepped from the cabin and stood looking uncertainly about her. In the high grass to her right a grouse flew up, and she started, clutching her cane tightly.

She feared the prairie with its strange sounds and long stillnesses. She had grown up in a town where one could hear the thud of a neighbor's ax, the drone of the sawmill, the ring of the ferry bell, the comforting sounds of other people. Here there was only the lonely sighing of grass bent by the wind.

"Dewey," she called again. Her voice was softer, for now, outside the cabin, she feared not only for the boy's safety but for her own. "Dewey! Answer me, boy, if you hear me!"

Hobbling slightly, she walked around the cabin toward the rise that overlooked the river. The dry prairie wind whipped her skirt about her thin legs. "Dewey! Dewey! Oh, where is that boy? *Deweeeeeee!*"

Her answer came from below on the river. "What do you want, Grandma?"

"Dewey Martin, I want you to get yourself up here right now. That's what I want. You hear me?"

"I'll be there in a minute."

"Right now!"

"I'll be there in just one more minute," he said. "I'm doing something real important."

"All right, you just stay on down there doing what's so important," she said, "and when your pa gets home and asks did you mind, I'm going to say, 'That boy never minded me at all. He was doing something too *important* to mind. He was—'"

"I'm coming, I'm coming."

"I ain't talking about coming in a hour or two. I want you right now."

Before she saw the boy, she saw his dog running up the path and she shook her cane at him and said, "Don't you upset me now, you worthless critter." The dog ran past her. He knew the boy was heading for the cabin, and there was no greater pleasure in his life than beating him to the cabin and being there to greet him in the doorway.

"I don't see you, Dewey," the woman warned.

"I'm right here, Grandma."

She was silent as he made his way up the path, and then she said, "Look at them feet." With her cane she pointed to the boy's feet, stained brown with mud from the river. He expected her to send him to the well with a gourd of soft soap. Instead she said, "What you been doing down at that river?"

"Nothing."

He ran into the weeds and up to the cabin. Brandishing her cane above her head, she made her way up the path. "I said, what you been doing down at that river? No good, I bet."

"Making something," he said over his shoulder. Then he came around the cabin, and the dog was there waiting for him in the doorway. His long tail was sweeping the cabin floor as hard as any broom. "Good dog, Charlie, good Charlie," the boy said, rubbing him, and then the two of them rolled on the floor.

"You act like you ain't seen him in a year," the woman grumbled at the door. With the aid of her cane she pulled herself into the cabin. "Don't upset me now," she said as she passed the boy and the dog. "That dog would rather upset me than eat meat." She fell into her rocker with a sigh. Carefully she patted her face with the hem of her apron.

"It ain't safe out there," she said.

"Pa wouldn't have left us if it wasn't safe," the boy said. The truth of this was absolutely clear to him: his father had said they would be safe, and so they would be.

"Well, maybe it was safe enough when he left," she conceded, rolling her eyes at him, "but that was four days ago and—mark my words—a lot can happen out here in four days." She rocked emphatically. "Wouldn't surprise me none if there was Indians all over the place by now."

"You seen any Indians?" the boy asked. He stopped patting the dog and sat up on the floor.

"Well, I ain't exactly *seen* any," she admitted, "but it wouldn't surprise me none if they was out there watching *us*. You don't ever *see* an Indian till it's too late." She stopped rocking and with her foot reached out and pushed the cabin door partially shut. "What was you doing down at the river?"

"Nothing."

She pointed at him with her cane and touched him on the shoulder with it so that he looked up at her. "I mean to know what you been doing down there every day," she said firmly.

"I said I was making something."

"All right then, what was you making?"

The boy laid his rumpled head on the dog. "I'm making me a sort of boat," he said finally, in a low voice.

"A boat? A boat?" she said. "I'd like to know where you're going in a boat!"

"Nowhere, I reckon. Just out on Trouble River. Anyway, it's more like a raft than a—"

"Trouble River," she said. Her disgust was plain. "That ain't no river. Wouldn't a fish be caught dead in that yellow water." She snorted. "A half mile wide and a half foot deep, that ain't no river. Why, I'd as soon eat mud as drink water from it." She leaned forward. Her finger, pointing at him, trembled slightly. "You can't even swim in it for the quicksand. I heard your pa say so."

"It's good enough for a raft."

"It ain't good for nothing. Nothing! It ain't even good for getting across. Whole wagons have gone down in quicksand trying to get across, I've heard tell."

"Not whole wagons, Grandma."

"That's what I've heard tell," she said stubbornly. "It'll suck the legs right off a horse." She leaned back in her chair. "That's how it come to be named Trouble River."

"It was named by some settlers who tried to cross after a heavy rain and lost their wagon. Pa said so."

"Well, anyway, you got no right to be out there making a boat when you got chores. All the things around here that need fixing, and you playing at making a boat. I never!"

"I knew you wouldn't like it," he said with his mouth partially buried in the dog's fur. "That's why I didn't want to say nothing."

His grandma rocked more slowly now, and the boy stared out the cabin door at the enormous moon in the sky.

"Your pa know about this here boat of yours?" she asked finally.

"Yes'm. He let me use the horses to haul the logs."

"Then he's just as fool as you are." She touched him again with her cane. "Don't you be getting in no trouble with it till your ma and pa gets back. You hear me?"

"Yes'm." He paused a moment and then said, "I wish I was with them." He closed his eyes. "I reckon they're in Hunter City now. If I was there I'd be with Jimmy Sayers and I could tell him about my raft. He didn't think I could—"

"Well, wishing ain't going to get you there," she interrupted, "or me either."

"I know."

"Somebody's always got to stay to look after the animals."

Dewey rolled over and put his face beside the dog's. Half asleep, the dog roused long enough to lick the boy's cheek. Dewey closed his eyes and thought of Hunter City with its buildings and tents. He thought of how it was to walk down the street and look in the tents and see men eating on long plank tables or gambling, of the sounds of the hurdy-gurdies and the laughter. He thought of walking among the canvas-covered wagons grouped by the river and talking to the emigrants, or standing in the back of the store and watching a checker game and munching on a hard kernel from the corn barrel. It seemed unfair that his parents were there where something was always happening and he was left back at the cabin where everything was always the same.

"It's dark," Grandma said. "Better bar the door."

The boy got up at once, pushed the door shut, and set the stout bar across it. Then he lay back beside the dog on the rough floor boards. He watched his grandma carefully. He was eager for her to go to bed, for he planned, as soon as she was asleep, to slip down to the river again. Tonight, however, she was wide awake.

"You going to bed, Grandma?" he asked finally.

"I ain't sleepy," she said. "I got a uneasy feeling."

He said nothing but began to pick a burr from behind the dog's ear. The dog waited patiently and then sniffed with great interest at the fur-covered burr which the boy held under his nose.

"I get these feelings sometimes," she continued. She stopped rocking and leaned forward in her chair. "When I was a girl we was eating supper one night and all of a sudden I got a feeling. Just sitting there at the table I got a feeling and I said straight off, 'Something's happened to Ben.'"

The boy rolled over on his stomach and looked at her.

"Ben was my brother," she explained.

"I know. And had something happened to him?"

She refused to be hurried. Her voice was quiet as she told the story. "Well, everybody laughed and carried on and made fun of me. 'What's happened to Ben?' they said. 'Did the Widow Cass get him?' They made fun of me. But I had this feeling all the same. I couldn't even eat; couldn't swallow. We got up from the table and I was wiping off the dishes and old Mr. Hunter come up the path. I can see him now because he looked like bad news. And he said to my pa, 'You better come with me, Jake. Ben's hurt.' And Pa went off with Mr. Hunter and when they come back they had Ben with them and he was white as death. His horse had throwed him and broke both his legs." She began to rock again. "Well, didn't nobody laugh any more when I got a feeling. I can tell you that."

"What kind of a feeling was it you had?" Dewey asked quietly.

"A scared feeling. I just felt scared." She paused. "And that's the way I'm feeling right now."

For the first time he, too, began to feel uneasy. He tried to calm himself with the thought that his father would not have left them alone if there was any danger. His father was a cautious man. That was why he had taken Dewey's ma to Hunter City to have her baby.

"Pa wouldn't have left us if it wasn't safe," he said stubbornly. "Last thing he said to me was that he knew we was going to get along fine." She did not answer. "He's left us before and nothing happened." He paused, then said, "He was gone more'n a week when he got the plow and didn't anything happen." He waited, looking up at her.

"All the same," she said, thumping her cane on the floor as she leaned forward, looking at him with her piercing eyes, "I got a feeling!"

Chapter 2

The Indian

It took his grandma a long time to fall asleep in her chair. She sat there working a buckskin, making it soft and pliable with her hands. Twice the skin dropped to her lap, but when Dewey stirred on the floor she straightened abruptly and said, "What was that?"

"It was just me, Grandma."

"Well, how come you don't go on to bed? You can't get no sleep down there on the floor." She rose from her chair as she spoke and moved to the window. The cabin was well built, the cracks chinked tight against the wind. There was real glass in the one window, and Grandma now hung a cloth over it. "There," she said.

"I'll stay up with you awhile," Dewey said, and with a faint nod, grateful for his company, she went back to her chair. She sat and her head was again bent forward over the buckskin. Dewey waited.

A screech owl cried behind the cabin. Dewey glanced quickly at his grandma, knowing she would say someone was going to die. That's what she always said when she heard a screech owl.

"Grandma?" he said quietly.

There was no answer. She was asleep at last.

He rose and moved in absolute silence to the door, but at once the dog shook himself and his ears flapped noisily against his head. Dewey winced. He drew his shoulders up and waited for his grandma to awaken and snap, What you up to, boy? But she did not stir.

Still without a sound, he lifted the bar and opened the door. The dog was outside first; the boy followed, pulling the door shut behind him.

He breathed deeply of the cool air. Usually he loved the prairie at night. It seemed to him that this was the way the ocean would look far out at sea. He glanced over the dark waves of grass that were almost moving in the moonlight, but tonight there was no pleasure in the sight. He was uneasy. His grandma had done it, he told himself angrily, talking about her "feeling." Now he was filled with dread, too.

He thought of going back into the cabin. He even lifted his hand to the door, but then he stopped, wishing suddenly he could be strong like his pa. His pa would never be frightened by an old woman's words. He would never stand here undecided, one hand raised to the door, one foot turned to the river.

Dewey took a deep breath and, glancing over his shoulder, started down the path. At the bank he paused to look down at his raft. He felt better as he looked at his handiwork. Dewey thought that it was the most beautiful sight he had ever seen.

As he stood there he had a brief, startlingly-clear picture of himself on the raft under the long, green shadows of the trees down the river. He saw his hands, broad and strong, gripping the oar and thrusting it into the shallow water, sending the raft over the water like a wind-blown leaf.

Smiling, he glanced over his shoulder again and then stepped onto the raft. It was made of nine logs lashed together with strips of hide and was approximately six feet across and eight feet long. Atop the logs Dewey had laid a floor of smaller split logs, nailing them so that they formed a platform. He had earned the money for the nails by picking up bones on the prairie and selling them in town. He had done all the work himself and he felt a pride that he had never known before.

It was the only thing he had ever made that was for himself alone. His family was almost machine-like in the way they worked to keep alive and comfortable, and sometimes Dewey felt that every hour of his day was taken up with the land and the animals; that he was part of the farm in the same way that the plow was, or the wagon. The raft was a separate thing, built only to give pleasure.

It seemed to him as fine as any of the rafts he had seen on the big rivers. Five years before, while waiting to cross the Mississippi, he had counted a string of a hundred and twenty rafts on its long journey to New Orleans. He had seen the low doghouses for the crew to sleep in, and a raft as big as a field with a tent for the family and fences for the horses and pigs. His was just as sturdy, just as ready to withstand the twists of the current as those.

He knelt at the front of the raft where he had put a large split log with the smooth side to the front. He took some stain he had made from old walnut hulls and dipped his finger into it and began to print across the front of the log. Slowly, carefully, ignoring the stain that was running down his finger, he began to print the first letter—*T.* He leaned back and looked at it and, not displeased, dipped his finger into the stain again.

A wolf howled in the night, and Dewey glanced up. The howl was far away, and after a moment he resumed his work. Once he had seen the wolves from the doorway of the cabin. They had sat in a half circle in the deep grass and howled in the moonlight, and when one wolf—the leader—had turned toward the cabin, his eyes had flashed green in the moonlight. Sometimes Dewey saw their tracks at the river and in the creek bottoms, but tonight they were far away, chasing elk and deer.

His hair, bleached pale from the sun, fell unnoticed over his eyes, and in the moonlight his tanned face was darker than his hair. The tip of his tongue touched his upper lip as he worked. Now he straightened and looked at the words he had printed. *The Rosey B.* The letters were even and again he felt a surge of pride. *The Rosey B* is a good ship, he thought as he looked her over, and now she was ready for her first voyage.

There was a noose of rope thrown over a stump on the bank to hold the raft to shore, and he slipped this off and coiled the rope at his feet. With mounting excitement, his fear forgotten, he bent and picked up the oar lying across the raft. This was his treasure. He had found it on the bank of Big River a year ago when he and his pa had gone over to get some wild plum trees.

"Pa, look, I found me an oar," he had cried. His pa had looked up, nodded, then gone back to working the shovel around the young plum tree.

"Can I take it home?" Dewey had stood clutching

the oar in his dirty hands, thinking of other people who might have held it—a dark Spaniard, a French hunter, an Indian. "It's a sturdy oar, Pa."

"Keep it."

"*Yahoo,*" he had cried. Putting his weight to the oar, he had swung a few feet off the ground before he had told his pa what he had thought the first moment he had seen the oar in the thick grass. "Pa, one day I'll make me a boat."

His pa had nodded.

"I'll make me a real boat and go everywhere."

And now he had his boat. Taking the oar, he jammed it against the muddy bank and pushed with all his might. He leaned on the oar, and slowly, heavily the raft moved into the water. It stuck on the muddy bottom, and Dewey pushed again. He could feel his head pounding with the effort. Then there was a certain lightness, an ease in the movement. He was afloat! For the first time he was afloat. He prepared to sweep the oar through the water. He had practiced many times on shore and he anticipated the powerful surge of the raft.

And then, abruptly, he froze. His hands clutched the oar to his chest. He did not move at all. He did not even breathe. For ahead of him, just up the river, he had heard the snort of a pony.

His father had taken both horses to Hunter City to pull the wagon, and there were no horses here now. A pony, he thought—an Indian. He waited. He made no noise. The raft slipped back against the bank and stopped. Still Dewey did not move.

The dog at his side sensed his caution, and he, too, was absolutely still. His ears, which usually flopped over his eyes like eyeshades, were now drawn back.

Carefully, silently, Dewey straightened. He looked

toward the cabin. His eyes searched the clearing, the grass beyond. Nothing. Still his mind repeated over and over again, a pony—an Indian.

He waited. Then, suddenly, he saw a movement in the grass to the left of the cabin. It could have been the wind, he thought, and then he saw in the moonlight the unmistakable gleam of a naked back. A fear clutched him so great that he felt as if he were spinning around and falling, and he was surprised to find, a moment later, that he was still standing on the raft, gripping the splintery logs with his toes.

The Indian, unaware that he was being observed, moved in a crouch around the cabin. His oily skin shone in the bright moonlight, and Dewey could see the tuft of hair on top of his head bound with cord, the animal furs that hung from a leather thong about his waist, the hatchet and knife stuck behind the leather thong, the bow, the shaft of arrows on his back.

Suddenly Dewey thought of his grandma. Again he heard his father's voice bidding him to take care of her. He heard his own confident words, "I'll look after Grandma same as you do, Pa." Slowly he put one foot onto the bank and balanced. Then he cautiously slipped the raft's rope over the stump. Without a sound, he lowered himself and slithered up until he could see the cabin.

The Indian was now approaching the barn. He disappeared into the shadows for a moment, and then Dewey saw the moonlight on his back as he opened the barn door. Dewey heard the sound of the sagging door scraping against the ground.

For a moment he felt easier. The Indian had come to steal the horses and the horses were safe in Hunter

City with his parents. He waited. A mosquito whined in his ear and Dewey brushed at his face.

The Indian looked into the barn and then moved across the yard with the silent ease of an animal. Dewey watched him approaching the cabin, and his moment of relief was gone as quickly as it had come. If the Indian was only after the horses, Dewey thought, he would leave now, move up the river to where his own pony waited. Instead he was walking toward the door of the cabin.

Dewey stepped to the top of the bank and then began to crawl up the path, the oar tight against his side. The dog followed behind him. Charlie had smelled the Indian now, and a low growl began deep in his throat. Dewey paused, bent, and, reaching backward, grasped the dog by the muzzle and squeezed to quiet him. The familiar feel of the dog comforted him and with a deep breath he continued up the path.

In the dry grass at the back of the cabin, Dewey crouched. He held the dog to him with one arm. He looked around the side of the cabin. The Indian was not in sight. Still in a crouch, Dewey moved closer.

There was something about the Indian's actions that troubled Dewey—the way he had moved about the clearing as if everything was familiar, the way he had glanced into the barn without entering. It was almost as if the Indian had known there would be no horses there, Dewey thought, and if he knew that, then he knew also that there was no one at the cabin but his grandma and him.

Now, suddenly, Dewey thought of the cabin door. He had left it unlocked! And just on the other side, sleeping fitfully in her rocking chair, was his grandma. Perhaps at this moment she was dreaming of Indians, and perhaps at this moment the Indian's hand was opening the door.

Forgetting his own safety, he started running toward the front of the cabin. Charlie let out a piercing bark and raced around the cabin too. The boy and the dog saw the Indian at the same time standing at the cabin door, hatchet in hand.

Without hesitating, the dog threw himself up on the Indian. His weight and the suddenness of his spring threw the Indian back against the cabin door. The dog's powerful jaws grabbed the Indian's arm, and he hung there a second, his teeth sinking into flesh. His body swung in the air. Almost at once the Indian dashed him to the ground, but he went for the Indian's feet, snapping wildly at the flesh just above the leather moccasin. His teeth pierced the Indian's ankle and held until he struck at him with his hatchet.

The boy was helping now, striking with his oar and screaming, "Pa, Pa, help, *Paaaaa*," forgetting that his father was far away in Hunter City.

The door of the cabin swung open, and the Indian waited to see no more. He ran with deerlike speed toward the trees.

With one leap Dewey was in the cabin. He thrust his grandma aside and grabbed the gun from the pegs over the door. He was trembling so violently that it took him two tries to cock the gun, and when he got to the door, the Indian was far away, riding his pony up the riverbank and out of sight.

Charlie had followed the Indian, but halfheartedly; the blow from the hatchet had severed the muscle of his right front leg, and it was now bleeding and useless. Panting, he limped back to the cabin and lay in the dust.

Holding the gun against his shoulder, Dewey looked over the horizon for some sign of the Indian, and it was then that he noticed the faint red glow to the north. It could only be a fire and Dewey thought of the Weiceks' cabin, which was in that direction.

The gun was suddenly heavy in his hands and he lowered it slowly and then looked again at the glow on the horizon. The dread that rose in him was so great his knees began to tremble and he clutched the door for support.

Chapter 3

Escape by Moonlight

"What happened? What happened?" Grandma asked, staring at Dewey with eyes that were dazed and uncomprehending. She had been awakened abruptly from her sleep, and she could not understand why Dewey had thrust her aside and grabbed the gun.

Dewey's chest was heaving so rapidly he could not speak for a moment. Then he said, "It was an Indian."

At the mention of the fearful word she stepped back. She sat down hard in her rocking chair. "Indians," she said starkly.

The dog whined and Dewey looked away from the horizon and at him for the first time. Then he stepped quickly from the cabin and picked him up. "Look at his leg, Grandma. He can't hardly walk on it." He set the dog in the cabin and closed the door.

Although his hands were shaking, he held a splinter in the glowing ashes of the fireplace until it flamed and then lit the oil lamp with it.

"Indians," Grandma said again.

The boy swallowed and wiped his nose on the sleeve of his shirt. "I got to fix Charlie's leg," he said, then added loudly, "Anyway, it was just one, Grandma."

She rolled her eyes to the ceiling. As the boy looked for cloth to bind Charlie's leg she said, "There ain't no such thing as *one* Indian."

Dewey paused. The glow he had seen on the horizon gave truth to her words. He pulled a piece of muslin from a drawer and began to tear it into strips. Now the urgency of looking after the dog began to replace his fear. "Maybe Pa'll be home in the morning," he said.

"Your pa won't be home for a week."

Dewey began to bind Charlie's leg to stop the flow of blood, and the dog whimpered and licked the boy's hand with his warm tongue. Dewey split one end of the cloth and wound it around the leg, then tied it in a knot. "Now lie there," he said, "and don't move around or you'll make the bleeding worse."

His grandma had begun to cry, not noisily, so Dewey did not notice at first, but when he glanced up from the dog's leg he saw the tears rolling down her cheeks. Unchecked, they fell to her blouse, and she made no effort to wipe them away.

Her tears upset him almost more than the encounter with the Indian. In all his life he had never seen a woman cry. He had heard his mother cry the night they knew his pa wasn't going to die with the fever, the night his pa had looked at her and for the first time in weeks had recognized her. But those had been happy tears. These seemed hopeless, and there was no sound at all.

"I only saw one of them, Grandma, and he's gone. He left on his pony."

She said nothing, did not even look at him, and the tears continued to slip down her cheeks.

"I said the Indian's gone," he said slowly. "We'll probably never even see him again."

She took a deep breath that rattled in her throat. "Oh, we'll see him again, him and a dozen of his brothers." She still did nothing about the tears.

"Don't say that." He had known this himself the moment he had seen the fire on the horizon, but he did not want to hear it. Then he said, "If they come back, we'll hide. That's it. We'll just hide, Grandma." Sometimes at night he thought about what he would do if raiding Indians came, and this was what he had decided. He would hide, flatten himself in the wheat and wait. Sometimes in the hot summer afternoons he had even gone and hidden to see how long he could remain absolutely still.

"There ain't no place an Indian can't find you," she said dully. "They got animal noses. They can smell you out."

"Well, it's better than just sitting here, ain't it? At least if we was hiding somewhere, we'd have a chance."

"We ain't got no chance, boy."

"We have, too, got a chance."

"No chance at all."

The suggestion that there was no hope for him made him furious, and he grabbed her hand. "We have, too, got a chance and don't you say anything different. I'll get some things together and we'll get out of here."

She did not speak. The fear of Indians had been with her since they came to the prairie. She never left the cabin without first scanning the waving grass for some sign of their presence. Indians had sometimes passed the cabin, lean and dusky on their shaggy, neglected ponies. They had come into the cabin and eaten corn cakes and deer before the fireplace, dropping on their haunches and never lifting their eyes from the hearth.

"They won't harm anyone," Pa had said again and again, and Dewey had looked at the Indians and believed him.

There were no words, however, that could lessen Grandma's fears. In her mind were the terrible stories of the Indian massacres, of families wiped out, of children stolen, of women scalped. These tales had been passed from cabin to cabin, had grown in the retelling, and now, in this wide-open prairie where there was no place to hide, they tormented her. Tonight, it seemed, all her fears were coming true.

She sat in her chair, dully watching him as he yanked a blanket from the bed, laid it on the floor, and began to pile things onto it. He took what food there was on the shelf, on the table, by the fireplace, and threw it on the blanket. Without looking at his grandma he tied the ends securely, and then crossed the room and picked up the gun.

"Come on, Grandma, we better—" and then he paused. He swallowed. "Grandma! Grandma!"

She sensed the urgency in his voice and feared the Indians were upon them. "Where?" she asked, half rising from her chair.

"Grandma, listen to me." He grabbed her hand. "We'll go down the river to the Dargans'. Grandma, we'll go down the river!"

She looked at him, right at him, for the first time. "What are you talking about, boy?"

"I'm talking about my boat. We'll get on it and we'll float down the river. Grandma, we can do it. I know we can."

"Down the river?"

"Yes'm, if we could get to the Dargans', they'd help us. We could stay there till Ma and Pa come back by."

"Yes, the Dargans would help us," she admitted.

"Then come *on*, Grandma."

She hesitated.

"All right then, *don't* come," he said, his voice rising. "Just sit there till the Indians come if you want to. Just sit there and wait for the Indians."

She stood up and reached for her cane in one motion. "I'll try it," she said. "I didn't come one thousand miles to have no Indian take my scalp. You get them things down to the boat and we'll get started."

He took the bundle, picked up his oar from the doorway, and moved awkwardly down the path. He flung them onto the raft and hurried back to the cabin.

His grandma was stepping to the door. In the time it had taken him to run to the raft and back she had gotten ready. Her bonnet, the white one with lace that she saved for special occasions was on her head, and in her hand was her velours satchel.

"I'll get the dog," he said. Charlie struggled to his feet and Dewey grabbed him around the middle. Without pausing he ran with him to the raft. "Wait there," he said, then ran back up the path to help his grandma.

"Don't upset me now," she cried as he ran toward her. She shook her cane at him.

"I won't, Grandma. I'll just take your satchel for you."

She handed it to him and said, "You take care with that, boy. Every valuable I've got in the world is in that satchel."

"Yes'm."

She looked back into the cabin, at the kettle on the fireplace, at the dough she had put on the hearth, at the clean bedding, at the cradle hollowed like a tiny dugout from a cottonwood log.

Quickly, while she was standing there, Dewey ran to the pigpens. He opened the first pen and shooed the pigs out into the clearing. "Git! Git! You, git now." The pigs, startled, moved out of the pen and stood looking back at him, snorting softly. He opened the pen where the two fattened boars had risen to their feet and were looking at him. "Git, you. Git!" Before his pa had left he had said, "When we get back, first thing we'll kill the hogs," and Dewey's mouth had watered at the thought of the juicy ham. "Git! You want the Indians to eat you? Git!" The red boars moved out of the pen.

Dewey opened the door to the sod barn and led out Brownie and her calf. By habit they turned slowly and started walking down the path to the fenced pasture by the river. "Git!" he said, waving Grandma's satchel at them. The cow and her calf quickened their pace, slowed as Dewey went back to the cabin, and then stopped.

"Come *on*, Grandma."

Carefully, one step at a time she left the cabin and made her way down the bank. So intent was she on finding a secure footing that she was all the way to the edge of the river before she got her first glimpse of *The Rosey B.*

"There she is," Dewey said proudly as he saw her look at the raft.

She didn't speak for a moment. She couldn't. The word *boat* had brought to mind a sturdy craft. She remembered the heavy steamboats of the Missouri with their upper decks loaded with wagons, the keelboats built to carry men and beasts, boats that would not tip or splinter no matter how swift the current. The sight of the log raft stunned her.

"This here's the boat?" she asked finally.

Sensing her dismay, he said quickly, "Well, it'll get us there, Grandma."

She closed her eyes for a moment. In the moonlight she seemed pale, washed of strength.

"Are you all right, Grandma?"

She opened her eyes, straightened her shoulders, and said, "I'm all right. Let's get—" she paused a moment and then said firmly, "aboard."

"Wait a minute, Grandma. Just wait."

He ran back up the path and into the cabin. When he returned he was carrying her rocking chair upside down on his head. This was the chair she had brought with her on the long trip west, strapped on the side of the wagon, and now she managed a faint smile.

"Grandma, you're going down the river in style," he said. "Like a lady on a steamboat." He set the chair in the center of the raft and, standing knee deep in the water, helped her aboard. She clutched his shoulder so tightly he thought his flesh would be bruised by her fingers. Then she was on the raft, sitting gingerly in her chair.

"I don't like it."

"I'll push off," Dewey said quickly, before she could decide to go back to the cabin.

He lifted the noose of rope from around the tree stump, dropped it on the raft and pushed slowly out from the bank. His feet were stuck in the loose, muddy bottom and as he drew them out he thought of the quicksand. He scrambled aboard.

The weight of his body caused the raft to dip momentarily, and his grandma cried, "Don't upset me, boy," and almost struck him over the head with the cane in her alarm.

"It's all right, Grandma, it's all right. See how steady we are now."

She placed her cane across her lap and settled back in her chair. "I want to tell you one thing, boy, before we get started."

"We're already started," Dewey said, watching the bank slip away.

She ignored him. "Before we get started, I want to say one thing. I didn't come no one thousand miles out to this wild land to be scalped."

"Yes'm, you told me."

"That's just the first part." She paused. "Also, I didn't come no one thousand miles out here to be *drowned* neither. Understand me, boy?"

"Yes'm. I won't drown you." He swallowed. "If I can help it."

"When I die, it's going to be in my bed and I'm going to be buried yonder by the plum trees with my feet pointing east so I can see the sun rising on Judgment Day. You hear me, boy?"

"Yes'm."

"All right then, we can get started now," she said. "But I tell you one more thing. I don't trust this here boat and I don't trust this here river. Ain't neither one of them anything to look at."

From the first moment she had seen Trouble River she had mistrusted it. It was nothing like the beautiful rivers in the East. Its waters were murky and discolored; from a distance it appeared to be yellow, on closer inspection, merely muddy. It was broad but not deep, with banks of sand or clay and only an occasional grove of cottonwoods for shade. The creeks that emptied into it were called Dry Gulch, Dead Man's Creek, Salt Run, Rusty Springs. These streams plus the ground water from the sand hills were all that kept the river flowing throughout the year. It was like a snake, moving slowly with coiling, twisting movements through the prairie grass.

Chapter

On the Unknown

For the second time that evening Dewey raised his oar. He steadied himself and then turned slowly and looked back at the cabin. He heard Brownie mooing at the pasture gate, and he could see the chimney against the starlit sky.

Turning quickly, he straightened the oar. The sense of being pursued was strong, and he wanted to send the raft flying over the water. It was this eagerness that made him stretch forward too far with the oar. "Here we go." He lost his balance for a moment, the oar slipped from his hand and fell with a splash into the water. Quickly he went down on his knees and grabbed as the oar floated just out of reach.

"Wait a minute," his grandma said in a hushed voice. "Don't start rowing yet."

"I won't." On his stomach he reached out his arms and sighed with relief as his fingers closed around the oar.

"I think I heard something," she whispered.

"It was just me. The oar slipped out of my hand."

"No, back there." She turned in her chair and at

once he straightened and looked over his shoulder too.

"What was it?" he asked.

"*Sh!*"

They waited. Slowly the raft drifted down the river. The wind had stopped and there was not even the sound of rippling water to break the stillness.

The sound came again, a trembling call and then a whistle that ran down the scale.

"There," she whispered. "Did you hear that?"

"That was a screech owl, Grandma."

"Not like any screech owl I ever heard. Indian maybe."

"No, an owl," he insisted. Surely the Indian could not have returned so swiftly, he thought. Suddenly he was cold with sweat.

He and Grandma listened without speaking. They drifted past a dark clump of cottonwoods and into an unsheltered stretch of water that made Dewey crouch lower on the raft. His grandma in her white bonnet seemed to tower above him.

"Get down, Grandma."

She leaned forward in her chair. The sound came again and they listened until the whistle faded.

"Sounds like an Indian," his grandma whispered.

"An owl."

"Well, if it *was* an owl," she said testily, "then it means somebody's going to die."

"That's just an old saying."

"Old saying, huh!" she said, still whispering. "I heard a screech owl the night Aunt Minnie died and I heard a screech owl the night Pearl Manning died and my mother heard a screech owl the night the earthquake shook the chimney off our house." She counted the incidents off on her fingers.

"Well, *we're* not going to die." He straightened enough to dig his oar into the river. It wavered as he pulled it through the water. Instead of the powerful surge forward he had anticipated, the raft turned slowly sideways so that his grandma was facing the bank.

"What did you do that for?" she whispered irritably.

He was as startled as she. "I'll straighten it." Still in an awkward crouch, he stepped around her chair, paddled in the opposite direction, then watched as the raft straightened.

His grandma was regarding him sharply with her small blackbird eyes. "We ain't got time to be spinning around like a top. Them Indians is liable to be on us any minute."

"I know."

"Well, let's get going."

He dipped the oar into the water in short, shallow strokes. For a moment the raft seemed caught in the water. He paddled deeply and the oar touched the muddy bottom of the river; he pushed, and the raft moved sluggishly forward.

"This thing don't seem to want to go," Grandma said.

Dewey paddled uneasily at the back of the raft. Even the gentlest of strokes seemed to make a splashing noise that caused him to cringe.

"Oh, it'll go," he said, "once I get a chance to do some paddling."

"*If* you get to do some paddling," she said darkly. She looked back as if expecting to see the Indians at any moment.

"Once we get around this bend up here, we'll be all right," he said, "probably."

"Huh."

"Anyway, that must have been a screech owl we heard back there. If it wasn't, by now we'd be—" He broke off quickly and began paddling harder.

"Be what?" she snapped. "Scalped?"

"Something like that," he muttered.

"If you ask me there ain't no something *like* getting scalped, except getting scalped." She straightened in her chair and settled her bonnet more firmly on her head.

The raft moved slowly along on the river. Now the water was shallow enough so that he could use the oar as a pole and push them along.

Grandma was silent for a while and then she said, "I hope, boy, that we ain't getting away from the Indians only to get ourselves into worse trouble."

"There's no worse trouble than Indians," he said.

"I mean I hope we ain't setting out on the unknown. I hope you know how far it is we got to go and that you know how deep this here water is and where the quicksand is at. You done a little investigating of this river, ain't you?"

"A little."

"We ain't just setting out on the unknown then?"

"Not exactly."

He thought, though, as he handled the heavy oar that that was exactly what they were doing—setting out on the unknown. He didn't know the river. He didn't know the raft. He wished that he had had time to experiment with both. He could do anything if only he had time to practice by himself. That was the way he had learned to shoot, and there was a pleasure in learning with no one watching. But now, with his grandma there, with her sharp eyes to notice every fault, every slip. . . . He continued to dip the oar into the water.

As they rounded a sharp bend in the river, the raft headed steadily toward the opposite bank and Dewey began paddling quickly.

While he paddled, drenching himself with water, he heard his grandma say, "You better steer it away from the bank yonder, boy."

"I am," he said through tight lips.

But his long, deep strokes seemed to draw them even more directly toward the bank he was trying to avoid.

"You better get to it, boy. You can't wait till just the last minute before you start turning it."

"Yes'm."

"A boat ain't nothing to fiddle around with."

"I'm not fiddling around."

Despite all his efforts, the raft continued to head for the bank. He moved around his grandma and jabbed the oar into the water, hoping to strike bottom as he had done before. But the water was deep here, and he waited, oar outthrust, until he could put it against the bank; then he pushed them back into the river's current.

"That's better," his grandma said without looking around. "Now keep it out here where it belongs. Don't fiddle around. There's currents in this river. I can feel them pulling at us."

"Yes'm."

"And I see we ain't getting very far very fast. Yonder's where we come to get the berries."

With her cane she pointed to the bank and Dewey looked up. It was true; they had made little progress for all his efforts.

"We don't go no faster than this, them Indians will find us come daylight. They don't call it Trouble River for nothing."

Quickly he began to dip his oar into the water, first on one side, then on the other. The raft rocked gently with his movement, riding easily in the water now. Dewey wondered suddenly if the Indian had already returned to the cabin, or even if the Indian was going to return. Perhaps he had been frightened and would never come back. Then this trip down the river was for nothing.

But Dewey knew the Indian would return. As silent as a shadow he would return with his brothers. They would move close about the cabin, unseen, unheard, till they circled it. Then they would fall upon it with frenzied whoops, invade it, burn it. This was the way it happened. Dewey had heard his parents speak of it at night when they thought he was asleep.

He glanced over his shoulder, then at his grandma, who now sat as straight and proper in her chair as if she were in her own parlor awaiting a caller. Charlie lay at her feet with his head propped on the log at the front of the raft.

Dewey could smell the pungent odor of the water as he moved the oar from side to side. His brows were drawn together. There was something uncertain about the river that worried him. At times there was a smoothness, a gentleness to the current, and then, around the next bend, the river would become strong enough to defy all his efforts with the oar.

An hour passed. Dewey shook his arms to ease the tension between his shoulders, and then abruptly he straightened. He looked to the left and in the moonlight saw the creek that emptied into the river. His hands tightened on the oar, for he knew this was Dead Man's Creek. Jimmy Sayers had brought Dewey here one afternoon and told him about it. In this creek, seven years before, the body of a man had been found leaning back against the bank as if he were asleep. The man, Jimmy Sayers said, had lost his wagon forty miles back on the trail when the axle broke. He had lost his horse at the creek—no one knew how that had happened—and then this man just sat down, leaned back against the bank, and died. There was no reason for it—he hadn't starved, he hadn't fallen, he hadn't been shot. He had just given up and died.

And Jimmy said, too, that at night when the moon was bright the ghost of the dead man hung like a white mist over the creek.

Scarcely daring to breathe, Dewey stretched tall and thought he saw, up the creek a way, hanging between the scrub trees like a hammock, the white mist.

"Yonder's Dead Man's Creek, Grandma," he said quickly, wanting to know if she saw it too.

She glanced to the left. "I'm glad to see you know the river, boy."

"Well, I don't know everything about it," he said. "Jimmy and I just rode Buck down here one day."

He rested his oar on the raft and leaned against it. His body was wet with sweat, and he felt cold and tired. The oar was heavy and his shoulders ached from the strain of holding it.

Gaining a little speed, the raft continued down the river evenly, and after a moment Dewey sank to his knees and then sat on the back of the raft. He was so tired he could no longer stand.

"What you doing back there? Ain't you going to steer no more?" Grandma asked, turning in her chair to look at him.

"I'll steer from down here," he said.

"I didn't know you could do it sitting down."

"Yes'm, it's just as easy sitting down as it was standing up."

"All right, only you keep at it. Hear me? You can't let up for a minute on a river like this one."

"Yes'm."

He rested his head on his knees. For a moment he watched the dark banks, the low masses of trees. He closed his eyes.

"Keep it good and steady," his grandma cautioned. She settled her satchel more firmly in her lap.

"Yes'm, I'll keep her good and steady."

No sooner were the words out of his mouth than he was asleep. It was a sleep so deep that he might have been in his own bed in the cabin, secure with his parents.

His grandma, unaware that the raft was at the mercy of the river, continued to give her instructions in a clear voice: "Good and steady. And mind them currents, hear me?" With her cane she emphasized her instructions, pointing the way tirelessly.

The hollow whistle of the screech owl sounded again, but Dewey did not hear it. Nor did he hear the words his grandma spoke over her shoulder. "Screech owl. Somebody's going to die."

Chapter 5

Aground

Behind her, Dewey slept for almost an hour and then he awoke abruptly. It was the sound of the raft scraping against the rocky bottom of the river that awakened him. He stood up quickly, put his oar into the water, and felt for the bottom. He pushed against the rocks with all his strength and the raft moved forward a few inches. Then it stopped again.

"Keep it moving, boy. A boat's like a wagon; you let it get stuck—it's stuck!"

"I'm trying."

He put all his weight to the oar. His muscles ached with the effort, but the raft remained where it was. With a sigh, Dewey stepped from the raft and into the cold, shallow water.

"Where you going?"

"I got to look around, Grandma."

"Are we stuck?"

"Yes'm."

"I told you."

With his lips held tight together he waded around the raft, then toward the far bank of the river looking for deeper water. The river was wide here and shallow. He struggled back to the raft, wincing as the rocks cut his bare feet.

"I didn't even think there *was* rocks in this here river," Grandma grumbled, "but you sure found them."

"I think I can get us moving again. There's deeper water over there."

"Well, let's get to it."

He swallowed. His feet were cold, his pants wet where he had stepped into a hole, his shoulders ached. He bent and tried to push the raft sideways. It was stuck fast. He moved to the front of the raft and pushed. Then he straightened and looked at his grandma.

"Grandma," he said, "I reckon you're going to have to get off the raft." He could imagine the sharpness of her expression as she took in this request.

There was a silence.

"Get off?" she said abruptly.

"Yes'm, just till I can get the raft on to deeper water."

She remained in her chair without moving.

"It'll be just a little way," he said, hoping it was true, "and the water isn't deep here. You can just walk right over to the bank there."

"When I got on this raft I wasn't expecting to *walk* all the way to the Dargans'," she grumbled.

"I know, Grandma, I wasn't expecting this either." He put his hand on the front of the raft and Charlie reached out and licked it. He scratched the dog's head and suddenly felt better. "Come on, Grandma."

Slowly, stiffly, she rose from her chair. "It don't suit me to walk."

"I know."

He helped her step through the shallow water to shore. On the bank she shook her wet skirt and dug her cane into the soft earth. She looked back to the raft where the dog sat watching them.

"Things is come to a pretty pass when the dog rides and the old woman has to walk." Then she turned and began to make her way around the low trees, as upset as a hen turned out of her nest.

Dewey hurried back to the raft. Without the weight of Grandma it was now higher in the water, and he began to push it sideways across the river.

It was not easy. Hampered by the darkness and by the fact that he was unfamiliar with this part of the river, he had to move slowly. Again and again he had to back the raft and move it toward the far bank to find deeper water.

He slipped, went down on his knees, then struggled up to guide the raft again. After a while he felt the water getting deeper and he called, "Grandma, I think it's all right now."

"I should think so. I've done walked half way to the Dargans'."

He paused. The moonlight was still bright enough that he could see her standing on the bank.

She said impatiently, "Well, come on over here and get me."

"I don't think I can."

"What?"

"If I leave the raft it'll start going on down the river, Grandma, and I can't bring it over there 'cause the water's too shallow."

"How am I going to get out there, boy?"

He paused again, swallowed, then said in a cheerful voice, "Just wade on out, Grandma."

She said nothing for a moment, then, "I got the only cobbler-made shoes in this here family—I've had these shoes five years, only I ain't going to have them no longer if I'm going to have to be jumping in and out of rivers all night, and wading this way and wading that way."

"A little water won't hurt your shoes," he said.

"I wouldn't call this a 'little' water," she grumbled.

They stood for a moment looking at each other. Then slowly, jabbing her cane before her, she stepped into the stream. "In all my life," she said as she walked unevenly on the gravelly bar, "I ain't never been asked to do nothing like wade in my good shoes. Twice!" She stumbled, paused to regain her balance, then continued so slowly Dewey could not tell whether she was moving or standing still. "Nobody has no respect for an old woman these days. 'Wade on out here, Grandma. Get off the raft and walk, Grandma.' Next thing it'll be, 'Get out and *push,* Grandma.'" With hesitant steps she made her way to the raft, and Dewey stepped down to help her on board.

"There!" he said when she was back on the raft.

"Yes, there!" she mimicked. "There is a pair of ruined shoes. There is a pair of five-dollar shoes that has walked one thousand miles without losing their shine and now they are ruined."

Already the raft was beginning to move forward again. Quickly Dewey climbed aboard and took up his oar.

"Well, I tell you one thing," she muttered. "I ain't walking no more. We can get stuck in mud and I'm sitting. We can get stuck on rocks and I'm sitting. I'm *sitting!* Hear me, boy?"

"Yes'm."

He sat down on the raft with the oar across his lap. He wanted to relax, to sleep again, but his hands were gripping the oar tightly, waiting for the next crisis. His whole body felt stiff in his wet, mud-encrusted clothes as he huddled behind his grandma looking from one bank to the other.

The raft continued on its way slowly and evenly, but still Dewey did not relax. The stars faded and the moon disappeared, and the thin light of dawn began to show the riverbanks, higher now and as sharp as if they had been cut away with an ax.

Sometimes, just before sunrise on the prairie, Dewey felt as if he were the only person in the world. There was a hush, a silence, a time when nothing moved. Now, as he trailed his oar into the dark, silent water, he felt the aloneness more than ever.

He turned to look as the sun, huge and red, began to rise like a flower coming up from the ground in full bloom.

"Well," his grandma said, "it's morning."

"Yes'm, it's morning."

"And look at that dog, will you?" she snapped. In the darkness Charlie had found the softness of the bundle and had curled up on top of it. "That's our food he's sleeping on, boy."

"Yes'm. Get off, Charlie."

Charlie opened his eyes and wriggled more firmly into the bundle.

"Charlie, get off now. Get off!" He prodded the dog with his foot.

Slowly Charlie unwound himself and stepped onto the bare raft, but his eyes, rolled to the side, were on the bundle, and after a moment he crawled back onto it and slept again.

Chapter 6

An Unexpected Stop

The morning seemed endless. It was like the long, dusty days coming west in the wagon when there had been nothing to see but more ground and more sky and nothing to do but keep moving. Dewey had had the feeling then that the wagon train was standing still despite the wheels that kept turning, and now he had the same feeling about the raft. They were moving—he had only to look at the banks and the water eddying around them to see that—and yet at times the raft seemed suspended in the river.

The chill of the night was gone, and the sun found them between the high banks of the river. They passed ash trees and cottonwoods but got only momentary relief in the patches of shade. Soon Grandma was fanning herself with the hem of her skirt.

"Hot," she said.

"Grandma, don't this remind you of coming out west in the wagon?"

"The creaking and jerking's the same but it ain't as

dusty," she said. Then she sighed. "Ain't we ever going to stop and eat, boy? I'm wanting to get off and stretch my legs."

"I'm looking for a place." The banks along this stretch of the river would be difficult for him to climb, impossible for Grandma. At last as they rounded a bend he saw the perfect spot—a grassy bank that jutted out into the water with a small tree that would help give support to her unsteady step.

His teeth clenched with the effort of turning the raft. The currents were strong, pulling the oar in the wrong direction.

"Why don't we stop yonder, boy?" his grandma said. She indicated with her cane the same place he had chosen.

The raft was agonizingly slow in changing direction, and when it finally did turn toward the point, it was too late. The edge of the raft struck the rock at the tip of the point, and this caused it to turn slowly around in the water. On the shore a small antelope watched them, its slender neck bent forward, its dark eyes curious but not afraid.

"What did you do that for?" his grandma snapped. "I thought we was going to stop there."

"No'm, not there."

"Well, where *are* we going to stop?"

"On down the river, I reckon."

"Well, let's stop this infernal turning." She was now facing in the direction they had just come from. "I like to see where I'm going, not where I've been."

"Yes'm."

He plunged his oar into the water almost fiercely. "There," he said.

"And remember that I'm wanting to stop. Hear me, boy?"

"Yes."

"Move the raft out of this here current and you won't have no trouble stopping. That's what I'd do."

They continued slowly down the river. Grandma began to slap one hand impatiently against the arm of her rocker. This continuous sound began to irritate Dewey, and when Charlie, who was restless too, began to whimper, he said harshly, "Hush up, Charlie."

"The dog," Grandma said slowly, still tapping her hand against the chair, "wants to get off this here raft."

Now they went through a long stretch of rocky shore with trees lining the river. His grandma could no more climb the rocks than the steep bank, he thought. On a distant hill, through the trees, he could see a long line of buffalo moving in Indian file. They stepped slowly, shaggy heads down in the deep, rank grass.

"Yonder's buffalo," he said.

His grandma did not even turn her head, but continued to slap her hand against the arm of her chair.

He watched as the buffalo seemed to sink, one by one, into the earth.

"You missed them. They must have gone down in a ravine."

She only slapped harder.

"Will you hush up!" he said tightly. She glanced at him and he added quickly, "Charlie," even though the dog was now as quiet as if he had given up all hope.

Ahead there was a bend in the river, and a long, low mudbank stretched out like a hand pointing to the opposite shore. It was so low in the water that

Dewey did not see it at first.

"You see that bank, don't you, boy?"

Now he saw it. "Yes'm."

"Well, steer on around it."

"Yes'm."

He put the oar into the water and paddled quickly. The raft turned slightly to the right, but it had gained speed in the long stretch of straight water, and Dewey could see at once that the raft was not going to clear the bank.

They drew closer, and Dewey knew they were going to hit. Rushing forward, bracing one foot on the low split log, he reached out with the oar to break the impact. Grandma sat forward in her chair to watch the boy's skillful maneuver that would send them around the bank and on down the river.

The oar jammed into the soft mud, then the other end punched hard into Dewey's chest, knocking him backward. Grandma, who was already leaning forward, was almost thrown out of her chair.

She straightened quickly and looked at Dewey from beneath her bonnet, her brows drawn close in annoyance. She stretched her neck up and she looked exactly like an eaglet he had once seen. "What did you go and do that for?" she asked testily.

He put one hand to his chest. He expected to find the imprint of the oar in his bones, and he breathed carefully. Nothing was broken. He sighed with relief.

"What are we doing here?" she asked.

"This is where we're going to stop," he said, setting the oar down beside him.

"Stop here?" She indicated the mudbank with her cane. "What are we stopping here for?"

Charlie, happy to have stopped at all, limped from the raft and then onto the mud bar to land, leaving a trail of staggered footprints behind him.

"Now, look at that," Grandma exclaimed. "The mud's soft. We can't walk on that."

Without a word Dewey secured the raft, took up the bundle, and slung it over his shoulder.

"More than likely it's quicksand," she warned. "Folks sink in quicksand and ain't never seen again."

He hesitated. "Charlie didn't sink."

"The dog don't weigh enough. You and me do."

Dewey moved to the edge of the raft and put his foot on the bank.

"If you sink, don't be hollering to me to save you."

As he stepped onto the bank he felt his foot begin to settle in the mud, and for a moment he thought it was quicksand. Then with a sucking noise his foot came free and he began to move quickly to shore.

Grandma looked at his footprints, now filling with water. "I ain't wanting to sink in no quicksand."

"Me either," Dewey said. "I'll be back to help you in a minute."

When he returned he was relieved to see that Grandma had risen from her chair and was preparing to step onto the mud. He took her arm, and the two of them slowly, noisily made their way to land.

"Oh, it's good to have ground under me," she said as she stepped ashore.

"I spread the blanket over here."

"Well, it ain't as bad as I thought. I never seen this nice little spot under the tree here."

He considered briefly saying that he *had* seen it and that was why he had decided to stop the raft at that precise spot, but the dull pain in his chest stopped him.

Wearily they sat on the blanket and looked over the supplies. The food, which had seemed ample to

Dewey when he was piling it into the blanket, now looked sparse and uninviting. There were a dozen or so raw potatoes, one tin cup, a jug of molasses, loose berries, a small pail that the berries had been in, two slabs of fried meat which had stained the blanket with grease, and several cakes of cornmeal which had crumbled.

"If you hadn't let the dog wallow all over the food," she said distastefully. She looked carefully over the possibilities.

"I couldn't help it—he just got on when I wasn't looking."

"He gets on everything," she grumbled, "and *in* everything. Well, hand me one of them cornmeal cakes, and get me some water in the cup, boy."

"Yes'm."

She took the cup of water he brought her and looked at it carefully for a moment to see if anything was stirring. Dewey ate a cornmeal cake slowly and watched her, knowing she was weighing her thirst against the danger of a cup of water from Trouble River. Then wordlessly she poured molasses from the jug into the water and looked at him.

"You ain't eating without blessing your food, are you, boy?"

He bowed his head quickly, aware of the dry cornmeal cake that filled his mouth.

"Lord," she began, "you see us out here in the wilderness. We are lost but we ain't scared, Lord, because we know that You take special care of anybody or anything that's lost. We thank you for this food and ask that it make us strong. Amen." She looked up. "Now you can swallow, boy."

He nodded. Rising quickly, he ran to the river, scooped up a handful of water, and drank. Then he filled the pail and came back drinking from it.

He ate without stopping, for he was hungry, and then he lay full out on the blanket on his stomach. "What if Pa comes home and finds us gone?" he said slowly.

"It ain't likely." She continued to sip the molasses and water, wishing it were hot potato coffee. "It's two days to Hunter City by wagon and two days back, and your ma'll want to rest up before she starts home with the baby. It ain't likely."

"But if there's trouble with the Indians, they'll hear about it, won't they?"

"Maybe," she said. She looked at him. "Only sometimes Indian trouble don't give any more warning than a snake. I seen a man get bit by a copperhead one time. He was loading stones to make a fireplace and a copperhead caught him right on the wrist, and there wasn't a sound of warning."

"But wouldn't people see the Indians coming? Wouldn't there be—"

"If there was fifty Indians, somebody might see them. Or if there was a hundred. Only Indian trouble ain't like that any more. There's maybe a handful of Indians, renegades, more likely than not, and they can move so quiet and quick you wouldn't see them even if you was looking right at them." She emptied the contents of her cup and then looked with distaste at the silt that was left in the bottom. "You heard about the trouble at Gibbon's Creek some years back?"

"Yes'm, Jimmy Sayers told me about it."

"And did Jimmy Sayers tell you how many Indians done all that killing?"

"No."

"Twelve. One dozen."

"But didn't the settlers have guns? Couldn't they have shot the Indians?"

"You can't shoot what you can't see, boy. Them Indians come up in the night and set fire to the cabins, one by one, and then when the folks come running out, the Indians shot them." She shook the cup at him. "If you hadn't seen that Indian, likely the same thing would have happened to us. He know'd there wasn't but a boy and an old woman in that cabin."

"Oh."

She set her cup in her lap and looked up at the sky. Dewey closed his eyes and the warmth of the sun made him drowsy. He heard his grandma unclasp the velours satchel containing all her valuables. She took out her marriage paper, old and faded, and set it aside. She took out a small blue bowl that she said was the very color of the hills back home. Then she reached into the bottom of the satchel and withdrew a small cloth bag. It was her button bag. Dewey had not seen it for years. She untied the cord and emptied into her lap the shower of buttons—glass, gilt, mother-of-pearl, heavy work buttons, round jet beads. Dewey fell asleep watching as Grandma looked at one button after another.

He felt he had been asleep only a moment when she took his shoulder and shook him. "We better get going, boy."

"Yes'm." He sat up and looked at the remaining food. He retied the blanket over the now pitifully small supplies, shouldered it, and lifted the gun to his other shoulder.

His back and side muscles ached, and he noticed the blisters on his hands. He was feeling the strain of the hours on the raft, but he was glad his grandma did not know this.

Still holding the blanket and gun, he paused and looked over the prairie. There was a haze on the horizon to the east, and he thought it might be smoke. Their cabin was in that direction.

"Grandma!" he said.

She looked at him. "What is it?"

His eyes, squinting toward the horizon, lowered suddenly. He had heard the anxiety in his grandma's voice, and he knew without looking that her face would be pinched with worry.

"Oh, nothing. Let's go."

"Is there anything wrong, boy? You don't see no Indians or nothing?" Her eyes were weak, and she took his arm tightly in her thin fingers.

"No."

"Well, what was you—"

"I thought I saw something but I probably didn't. Come on."

She paused a moment, then lifted her head quickly, the way an old mare does in the spring, and followed him, holding tightly to his shoulder.

Chapter 7

Tragedy in the Ashes

When they were back on the raft, and Grandma in her chair again, Dewey poled the raft around the mudbank and into the mainstream of the river.

"Steady, boy," Grandma said.

"Yes'm."

After a moment he was aware that Grandma had no further instructions for him, and he looked and saw that she had fallen asleep.

Silently they drifted down the river. They passed a long treeless bank and Dewey could see the golden stretch of grass beyond and the streaks of red sumac that laced it.

Now he began to think of the Dargans. He had just passed the high clay bluff he had noticed often from the trail, and the Dargan cabin was not more than an hour or two away. He must stay awake and alert. It would not do to pass it by. He moved the raft closer to the left bank so that stopping would not be a problem.

The Dargan family had been here on the prairie longer than any other family, and Mr. Dargan, a tall, strong man with a beard that reached to his belt buckle, would take them in as warmly as if they were his own kin. In his mind Dewey could hear Mr. Dargan's voice, welcoming but concerned, saying, "Come in, come in. Margaret, get Mrs. Martin and Dewey something hot to drink." And drawing him aside he would say, "All right, Dewey, lad, tell me what the trouble is." What a relief it would be to tell of their trouble and place the responsibility on broader shoulders.

He watched the left side of the river eagerly, for he was afraid that the cabin would not be visible from the river. It was set back in the shelter of another smaller bluff: Chimney Bluff it was called because of the high stack of rocks on the top. It was this pile of rocks that Dewey was watching for.

He thought of the good hot supper Mrs. Dargan would fix for them—his cold lunch felt like a hard knot in his stomach—and he thought of the soft sweet-smelling grass mattress in the loft. He and his grandma would stay until his parents came by on their way home. His pa and ma always stopped at the Dargans', and then the four of them could ride home together—five now, with the baby.

His eyes burned from the glare of the water and from lack of sleep, but he continued to look for the bluff. He felt a heightening of spirits now that the journey was nearing its end, and he allowed himself to whisper excitedly to Charlie, "We'll be there in just a bit."

The dog had begun to pull at the bandage that bound his leg as if that were the cause of his pain. Dewey put down the oar, tied the bandage more securely, and said again, "We'll be there in just a bit."

The words did not comfort the dog, but they made

Dewey feel better. He straightened and began to whistle.

With a start, his grandma awoke. "How long did I sleep?" she asked anxiously.

"A couple of hours."

"Did you get along all right?"

"Yes'm."

"I was afraid you might have run into some trouble."

"No'm, I did all right."

"Seem like we ought to be seeing the Dargan place before long," she said. "I brought along my crocheting so Mrs. Dargan could get me started on a new pattern." Already she, too, pictured herself in the cabin, happily chatting with Mrs. Dargan. "You know it ain't been a bad trip, boy," she said. She smoothed her skirt, then straightened her collar and bonnet.

"No, it ain't," he agreed.

"Maybe you can bring me down the river again sometime next spring," she said. "We could come down, spend a night or two with the Dargans, and then go home."

"Yes'm." Dewey did not spoil her plans by mentioning that the raft would not go back up the river. It was a thought he himself did not like. At the Dargans' his raft would have to be abandoned, and he would never have those long, happy hours at home with it.

"Ain't that Chimney Bluff, boy?" With her cane she pointed ahead where a tall pile of rocks could be seen angled awkwardly against the hard blue sky.

"That's it." He dipped his oar into the water, and then paddled in short, nervous strokes on the right side of the raft.

"Get ready to stop, boy."

"Yes'm."

"Only wait till we get closer."

"Yes'm."

"I'll tell you when to stop."

"Yes'm."

He poled the raft closer to the shore. He could see wild blackberries on the vine and a tiny green snake hanging over the water, its head lifted to watch their passing.

"Don't miss the bank, boy."

"I won't," he said loudly.

Although the raft was now out of the current and moving slowly, Dewey was still tense. His hands gripped the oar so tightly that his knuckles showed white beneath his tanned skin. He dipped the oar again and again into the water, nervously marking time. His mud-stiffened breeches scratched against his legs.

He was so close to the bank that he could not see the cabin at all, but when his grandma said, "Now, boy!" without hesitating he thrust the raft into shore and grabbed the weeds on the bank with his free hand. They bumped against the bank and stopped.

Dewey leaned weakly on his oar for a moment, then he said, "I'll take her down there to that stump."

Slowly he let the raft glide the few yards and secured it with the rope. "We're here," he said.

His grandma stood up and looked at the weed-covered bank. "Can't you take us where it ain't so steep, boy?"

"You wait here, Grandma. I'll go up and get Mr. Dargan."

"Yes," she agreed eagerly. "Tell Mr. Dargan to

come down here and help me up the bank. Now, don't fiddle around, boy. Get him straight away."

"Yes'm."

"Don't stop to play or nothing."

"I won't, Grandma," he said impatiently.

He scrambled up the bank with his hands clutching the long weeds for support. At the top he stopped to look down at his grandma sitting erect in her chair. As he paused he saw her reach into her satchel and take out her gold-rimmed spectacles. These were her most prized possession. She often said she was the only woman west of the Mississippi who had gold-rimmed spectacles. Now she put them on, carefully hooking them behind each ear. She glanced up at Dewey through the small glass circles, and he said quickly, "I'm going right now."

The prairie wind, warm and gentle, blew against him as he ran toward the low trees that surrounded the Dargans' cabin. His hair tossed in the wind, and he ran gayly, happy that the journey was over and that he and *The Rosey B* had stood up to it.

Behind him the dog limped on three legs, straining to keep up. It was unbearable for him to have to run behind the boy when he had always been the leader—first up the path, first in the cabin, first to see what was over the hill. He barked his displeasure once, but Dewey did not wait for him. His bare feet flashed in the grass, and a prairie chicken scuttled out of his way.

"Mr. Dargan, Mr. Dargan," he called.

As he came closer to the trees he began to run more slowly. Then he walked. Then he stood perfectly still, not even aware of the grass blowing against his legs, for suddenly he had the feeling that something was terribly wrong. It was such a strong feeling that he wanted to turn and run back to the raft without going to the cabin at all.

There was an unnatural stillness beyond the trees. No one answered his call. No smoke curled up from the chimney, yet there was the smell of it in the air.

Slowly Dewey walked to the trees. His throat was so dry he could not swallow. He pushed through the low branches and what he saw in the clearing ahead made him close his eyes and hold tightly to a tree.

There, before him, lay the blackened ruin of the cabin. The logs, once sturdy and straight, were now charred and fallen, and the ashes had been scattered by the wind so that the earth, too, was black. Only the chimney, still high and strong, was left to show that what had been there was a cabin.

Dewey walked forward. He stepped to where the entrance had been. The hinges Mr. Dargan had brought from their old home in Virginia were there, still hanging from a log.

Dewey knelt and felt the log, turned it, and felt it again. Beneath, there was still a faint warmth. The cabin had been burned about two days ago, he guessed, and he suddenly felt cold with fear. His pa and ma! If they had stayed here an extra day, only one extra day, they would have been trapped with the Dargans.

He rose slowly as he surveyed the whole of the ruins, looking with dread for some sign of his parents. His shoulders suddenly felt heavy and tired as if he were carrying an unbearable burden. The barn was gone, burned like the cabin, and the horses—the fine mustangs—were nowhere to be seen. There was nothing but charred wood and ashes.

"*Deweeeee.*"

"Yes'm," he answered in a voice that was barely audible even in the clearing.

"*Deweeeee.*"

"I'm coming," he called.

The dog was sniffing in the ruins, running eagerly from place to place, poking his nose into the ashes. "Come on," Dewey said. "Come on, Charlie." Charlie ignored him and sniffed the ground. "I said for you to come on and I mean it. Now, *git!*" He picked up a bit of wood and threw it at him. The dog dodged awkwardly on three legs and looked at Dewey. "Now, *come on.*"

Reluctantly the dog followed. As they left the clearing, the ashes blew against their legs. Dewey did not look back. He crossed the meadow slowly with his eyes on the ground. His face was pale, and there was a white circle about his lips. As he walked, suddenly the sky above him was streaked with geese flying south. The sound of their honking calls filled the air, but Dewey did not even look up. He walked, the dog at his heels, toward the river.

His grandma heard his footsteps and she said eagerly, "Over here, Mr. Dargan. I'm over here." Then, "Is that you, Mr. Dargan?"

"No'm, it's me," Dewey said.

He stood on the bank for a moment, and she looked up into his face, pinched and small above his faded shirt. She was silent. She knew at once something was wrong, but her mind could not accept what it might be.

"Where's Mr. Dargan?" she said finally.

He did not say anything for a long moment. He looked down at his bare feet. Then he said, "The Dargans ain't there."

Now she read the truth in his face, and she closed

her eyes and her chin crumpled like thin paper. Her hands trembled in her lap. But when she spoke, her voice was almost steady. "Well, that's a shame," she said. "I'm real sorry we don't find them at home."

"Yes'm." He was grateful she was going to pretend that nothing was wrong. He could not have told her what he had seen, and now, in the cool shelter of the trees, it seemed almost not to have happened.

"I'm just disappointed because I was needing some help with my crocheting," she said, as if to explain the tears she was brushing from her cheeks.

"I know you was."

"Well, don't just stand there, boy. Get back on the raft. If the Dargans ain't at home, we'll just have to keep on down the river."

He grabbed the dog, who was looking back toward the cabin, and slid down the bank with him.

Without a word he got back on the raft, unhooked the rope, took up his oar, and pushed the raft out into the river. Both he and Grandma were silent as Chimney Bluff slipped from sight. Then with great care his grandma took off her gold-rimmed glasses and put them back in her velours satchel.

After a moment she said, "You didn't see no signs of your pa and ma, did you, boy? The wagon or the horses?"

"No'm. I didn't see much of anything."

"I reckon they're already in Hunter City then."

"They're probably having themselves a fine time right now," he said with false cheerfulness. He would not even let himself think that his parents might have been in the Dargans' cabin when the Indians came. They were in Hunter City. They had to be.

Chapter 8

Wolves

At dusk they stopped in the shelter of an old, dry creek bed. There was a widened sandy place where a pool had once formed, and Dewey set his grandma's rocker on it and then spread his blanket on the rise above it.

They ate what was left of the cornmeal cakes, some fresh berries that Dewey gathered from nearby bushes, and drank water sweetened with molasses. Dewey washed two of the potatoes in the river and offered one to her, but she shook her head. "My teeth can't chew no raw potato," she said. Kneeling, Dewey ate one and washed it down with water.

With the flat taste of the potato in his mouth, he suddenly remembered the geese in the sky, and he wished for a goose roasting over a fire, the way his pa had fixed them last spring. "Roast goose would be good," he said, unable to keep the painful thought to himself.

"And so would a good bed, but we ain't got neither." She had been thinking of the fig tree that grew in her yard when she was a girl, and she had been wishing that she could have just one of those sweet, sun-warmed figs. "Try to get some sleep," she said abruptly.

"I don't think I can."

"Well, stretch out there on the blanket."

"Yes'm."

He had been sitting on the edge of the blanket, drawing a stick through the pale sand, and now he turned. Charlie was curled up in the center of the blanket so Dewey lay beside him. He was so tired that his body ached, but he could not sleep. He lay with his hands locked behind his head.

He wanted to build a fire, a small one of twigs and the litter of dry leaves, and he wanted to sit during the night feeding the fire. There would be comfort in this small task, but he dared not risk the smoke that would mark their presence.

After a moment he said, "I think the Dargans are dead." It was not what he had meant to say at all, and he wished he could take back the words.

His grandma tried to set her chair in motion, but it would not rock in the soft sand. Then she stopped and said, "Sh, boy. Try not to think about it."

"I can't help it."

She sighed. "I know. I was sitting here thinking of it too."

"How come the Indians killed them?"

She shook her head. "Indians," she said. "I don't know, boy. Something gets into them, some hurt, some fear, and they just strike out."

"But why the Dargans?"

"I don't reckon it was anything the Dargans did, if that's what you're thinking. There wasn't a kinder man anywhere than Mr. Dargan. Them days that your pa had the fever—why, we couldn't have kept going if it hadn't been for him." Her eyes rolled up to the darkening sky. "More than likely them hunters from the north that killed that squaw last spring was what started it."

"But that was an accident."

"Well, it wouldn't be the first accident that's started trouble. I ain't saying for sure that's what it was, I'm just saying it could be." She sighed. "Don't nobody understand really. Now, try and get some sleep."

"Yes'm." He reached off the blanket, picked up a clod of earth, and broke it in his hand. He had seen his father kneel and do this many times in a plowed field, and he realized suddenly that it was not food he wanted at all, not even roast goose. It was his father. Abruptly he wiped his hands on his breeches.

"And push that dog off the blanket," his grandma said. "I swear that worthless thing'll be up in my chair next."

"He's all right, Grandma." He hugged the dog to him. He had the lonely feeling that he and Grandma and Charlie were the only living creatures left in the world, and he buried his face in the dog's fur and waited until the tears in his eyes had dried.

"Grandma," he said after a while.

"What is it now? I thought you was asleep."

"I was just wondering, Grandma, what's going to happen to us. I mean, if our cabin's burned." The thought had been troubling him all afternoon. The urgency of saving their lives had made the cabin seem unimportant at first. Now, suddenly, it was the most important thing in the world.

"Well, I don't reckon it'll be the first time people has had to build again."

"But—"

"If you get the *chance* to build again," she said slowly, and he knew she was thinking of the Dargans, "well, you thank the Lord and do it."

"Yes'm."

"There was a man back home got burned out twice—last time he was scalped and left for dead. It was a pitiful thing."

"What did he do?"

"He built again. He built right on the spot where his first cabin had been. Twice. And he lived on that spot till he was ninety-one years of age."

He was silent for a moment. "What did he do about his head though, Grandma?"

"He wore a handkerchief over it and, as far as I know, forgot about it," she said sharply, as if she were disappointed by the question. She paused and Dewey thought that was all, but then she said, "There is something inside a person—I don't know how to give it a name exactly—but when something bad happens to you, like your Uncle Ben breaking both his legs, or your ma having two little babies in a row that never drew a breath, well, a person thinks, This here's the end. I've thought it. I thought it when I had to come live out here on the prairie. I crawled up in that wagon and I said to myself, 'This here's the end.' I reckon you'll think it more than once in your life. Only then a little time passes, a week or maybe it takes a year, and this something inside a person—whatever you'd call it—makes you come alive again."

"I wonder if I'd be like that man," Dewey said. "I don't think I could rebuild a cabin twice."

"You could if there was anything to you at all," she said, suddenly brusque. "Now get some sleep. You can't be steering us into Hunter City tomorrow if you don't get some sleep."

"I'll try." He shifted restlessly. He wanted to ask her how you knew if there *was* anything to you at all; how you knew *before* something bad happened. Maybe, he thought, I would be like the man in Dead Man's Creek who just gave up and died because his wagon and horse were gone. "Grandma?"

"Go to sleep."

He lay on his back for a long time, looking up at the sky. When sleep finally came, it was troubled. Hordes of Indians rode in his dreams, chasing the raft, and the raft moved with agonizing slowness on the water. The Indians were gaining on them, moving closer and closer, and the raft would not move. He rowed so hard the water rose behind them as if on a paddle wheel, and still the raft would not go forward. The Indians were coming closer.

He awoke, wet with sweat in the chilly air, and then he realized that it was not the dream that had awakened him. Charlie had risen on the blanket and was looking up into the darkness, a low, menacing growl deep in his throat. His teeth showed white beneath his raised upper lip.

The Indians, Dewey thought. Without a sound he reached for the gun he had brought ashore with him. For a moment he could not find it and then his hand curled around the wooden butt of the gun and he raised it against his chest.

Silently he sat up and put it to his shoulder in one motion. Then he turned and glanced up. He saw nothing but the bushes, dark and jagged above him.

This had seemed the ideal spot to camp when he had first seen it. It was sheltered and protected, but now Dewey realized that it would be easy for an enemy to slip up on them under cover of the brush.

Dewey waited. He could see nothing. And then from the bushes above he heard a snarl and the rising, sinister howl of a wolf. He clutched the gun and said in a low voice, "Grandma, wake up."

"What? What?" she said. She awakened so abruptly that her cane jabbed deep into the soft sand.

"Grandma, I think there's wolves up there."

"Wolves!" she said. She was fully awake now, for she feared them perhaps more than Indians. As a child her fear of wolves had begun with her first fairy tale, and now she gasped, "They'll eat us alive." Her voice was helpless and old, and her hands clutched the arms of her rocker so tightly that the veins stood out like vines on pale sand.

"Hush, Grandma. I got the gun."

"Well, shoot then," she gasped.

He watched, the gun to his shoulder, and suddenly through the darkness he saw the first wolf. It darted through the bushes and paused, snarling above them. Its slavering jaws were pulled back to reveal its fangs, and his grandma said again, "Shoot!"

Charlie growled, stepped forward, forgetting his wounded leg, and stumbled on the blanket.

At once the wolf came closer. He lunged as if to leap upon them, then withdrew, lunged again, testing the strength of his prey. Behind, eyes catching the gleam of the moonlight, other wolves moved back and forth, waiting to attack with their leader. From time to time they howled and showed their dark faces through the brush.

Dewey pointed the gun at the first wolf.

"Shoot," his grandma said again. So firm was her command that he almost pulled the trigger in spite of himself.

In the ragged shadows, the wolf, snarling and

threatening, advanced to the brim of the creek bed. He paused and then, with a frenzied growl, crouched to jump.

Dewey fired. The butt of the gun rammed into his shoulder and he fell backward with the force of the recoil. The wolf turned and disappeared, and Dewey heard the rustle of its body as it stumbled in the dry brush, rose and ran again.

There was a confused mingling of yelps, snarls, and the cry of the wounded wolf. Dewey said quickly, "Let's go."

He took his grandma by the arm, and with the other hoisted the unwieldy rocker. "Charlie," he said firmly, "come."

The dog wanted to give chase. He moved toward the bank and looked up to where the wolves still moved, confused over their wounded leader.

"Charlie!"

Reluctantly, Charlie followed the boy as he stumbled toward the raft under his load.

"Help me, boy," his grandma gasped. She clutched his arm and her cane in the same hand, and the cane pressed painfully into his flesh. From her other hand the velours satchel swung like a wild thing. "Help me!"

"I am, Grandma. I am."

He threw the chair on the raft, and before she was seated began to push the raft away from the shore with his oar.

"I ain't set yet," she said. Then, "But go on, boy, go on."

On the shore a wolf howled, a high, lonely sound, and then the other wolves took up the chorus; they ran in a pack to the bank and started for the raft, reaching out over the water with open jaws.

Charlie barked sharply. He stood on the edge of the raft, crouched as if he were about to jump into the water and swim for the hateful beasts now taunting him with their howls on the shore.

One wolf waded into the water, and Dewey drove it back with his oar. Quickly he brought the raft into deep water.

"Oh!" said his grandma with a sigh. She rose slightly and shifted her chair to the center of the raft. "Oh!" She touched her cheeks with her hands as if to cool the fevered fright that burned there. "Don't stop no more, boy," she said finally. "Whatever happens, don't stop no more. Them awful wolves."

"Wolves ain't so bad, Grandma. Pa says they're cowards."

"Not in a pack they ain't," she said. "I'd rather come on a bear than a pack of wolves."

"Not me."

She brushed at her skirt. "Oh, you can charm a bear by humming to him, if you know how," she said. "Once when I was a girl I was out picking berries and I come on a bear. A big bear it was and black as night. Well, I remembered how my uncle told me about charming bears and I started singing. I was never so scared in my life. I sang and I sang. One blow of that bear's paw and I wouldn't be sitting here today. Well, I can tell you, I *sang*."

"And what happened?"

"Well, that bear he never moved, never took one step toward me. And after a bit—still singing my head off—I picked up my bucket real slow-like and walked backward all the way down the hill. And the last I seen of that bear he was standing there looking after me and listening to me singing."

"What did you sing, Grandma?"

"What did I sing? Every song I knew of. 'Pig in the Parlor' and 'Hush the Baby,' and when I ran out of songs I made some up." She turned and looked over her shoulder. "But wolves! You try singing to a wolf and see what it gets you."

"I reckon it wouldn't do much good."

"That's why I say I don't want to stop no more till we are inside Hunter City."

"I can keep going if you can, Grandma."

"Reckon how much farther is it?"

"I don't know."

"The Dargans' place was about halfway, wasn't it?"

"By land. I don't know how far it is by the river. I don't even know nobody that's gone to Hunter City by the river."

Trouble River wound through the prairie like an animal on the scent of its prey. It hurried, then slowed, it twisted, then straightened, turned again and again, hooked, and at last, after its long and twisted journey, began to gain speed before it would rush headlong into Big River, mingling its brown water with the green of the larger river. There, at the joining of the two rivers, would be Hunter City.

"Seems like we're picking up a little speed, don't it, boy?" she said, and her voice was lighter. "Maybe we'll get there by morning."

"Yes'm."

"Only don't you let us get going too fast, hear me, boy?"

"I can slow it down when I want to." He stuck his oar behind him into the water. They rounded a turn. "This here's a crazy river."

"It's getting us there though, boy." His grandma

could not bear to hear a friend criticized.

Dewey smiled. He dipped his paddle into the water and again began to feel the glow of confidence. He felt that the worst of the journey was over. They had escaped the Indians and the wolves, and at any moment—surely by morning—they would be in Hunter City. He had no way of knowing about the stretch of treacherous water that lay ahead.

Chapter 9

The Rapids

Dewey kept his eyes on the shores of the river. He was afraid that Indians, if they were in the area, would be drawn by the sound of the gunfire. In the moonlight he occasionally saw the wolves slinking on the shore, but it did not trouble him. As long as he kept the raft in the center of the river, he and his grandma would be safe from them.

He poled the raft closer to the far bank.

"Keep it steady, boy," his grandma said. "Ain't no time to be upsetting now that we're most there."

"No'm."

Charlie had given up growling at the wolves and now sat uneasily by Grandma's feet. The blanket had been abandoned in the rush for the raft, and now he had nothing to lie on. The water licking between the logs made him uneasy. He stuck his cold nose up into Grandma's hand.

"You worthless critter," she said. "You think I got nothing better to do than to hold your nose?" Still she patted his head before she withdrew her hand. "I reckon we'll all be glad to see friendly faces, the dog too."

"He ain't a bad dog, Grandma. It was him scared the Indian off back at the cabin."

"I know," she said, softening. Then, "Only he just likes to make such a nuisance of himself. Look at him there—making himself comfortable on the hem of my skirt. Worthless critter!"

Charlie looked up, licked at her with his long tongue, and wiggled closer. Although she would not admit it, the warmth of the dog felt good against her legs, and she did not make him move.

"Maybe by now everything's gone wrong that can," Dewey said hopefully.

"Maybe."

"There's lots of things to go wrong out here. More than back in Ohio," Dewey said. "Indians and wolves, everything."

"It ain't only out here. The year I was five years old, now that *was* a year for things going wrong. I heard my ma tell about it again and again. First the river flooded. Then there was hailstones big as nuts that beat down all the crops. Then come earthquakes that shook down whole houses—the chimney just fell right off our house in the middle of one night. There was gray squirrels, thousands of them, coming through the country like the wind and strange lights in the sky. It was a fearful time my ma said. Folks thought it was the end of the world. Only here we are still going on and on."

An island loomed ahead of them, a flat piece of land strewn with old timber and matted growth. The raft touched on the edge of the island, then swung slowly around and continued sideways down the river. Quickly Dewey straightened it.

"Don't nothing come easy nowhere," Grandma said.

"I reckon."

Now they fell silent. Only the sound of Dewey's oar dipping into the water broke the silence. Dewey had no idea of the time. The moon was dropping in the sky, but there were no morning sounds and he knew daylight was still hours away.

He bent to reach under the raft, feeling the strips of hide. Some of them had begun to fray because of the constant rubbing of the logs, but he thought there was no danger. The raft would see them through.

His grandma began to hum, then sang softly in her high voice:

> Thirteen years I traveled,
> Thirteen years I roamed,
> Thirteen years I traveled,
> And now I'm going home.

When he was younger she would sing to him every night before he fell asleep. He had thought her voice as beautiful as a silver bell, and then one evening he had said impatiently, "I ain't a baby no more, Grandma; you don't have to sing to me," and she had not sung again.

Now, as they drifted down the river, for the first time in years he had heard her sing again. Her voice was older, thinner, but painfully familiar as she sang the song of the weary traveler far from home. He sang with her on the last chorus:

> No more will I travel,
> No more will I roam,
> No more will I travel,
> For I am going home.

Their singing was quiet, and when they finished they fell silent again, each lost in thought. Dewey looked at his grandma's back, so straight and proud, and at the white lace-edged bonnet which hung over the back of the chair. Removing her bonnet had been the only concession to the difficulties of the trip.

He shifted position and began to rub some of the stiffness out of his arms. His bare feet were cold against the wet logs, and suddenly he wanted to be in Hunter City so badly that his knees began to tremble. He dipped his oar deep into the water to speed their progress.

By dawn they were gaining speed again. The river had straightened, and the water, as if released from its confining path, rushed toward its goal, Big River.

"Maybe you better slow us down, boy," Grandma said. It was the first she had spoken in hours though she had not been asleep. "It ain't that I don't want to get there fast as you do."

"Yes'm, I will."

"It's just that I don't want to get upset."

"I'll slow her down." He plunged his oar into the water, bracing himself, and waited for the raft to slow, but this seemed to have no effect. The raft traveled on the water as if borne by a billowing sail.

"Slow her down." Grandma jabbed her cane into the air. "Now, boy."

"I am," he said. Again he swept the oar against the current, then added in a low voice, "Much as I can."

She glanced back at him, and he tried not to show his concern. "We'll slow up in a bit, Grandma. If we don't, I'll stop when we get up beyond them bluffs."

The river had swung to the east and the sun was shining directly into his eyes. He squinted and lifted his hand to shade them.

Ahead, on either side of the river, bluffs rose tall and rocky. Dewey thought briefly of landing the raft, but the shore was ragged with boulders; he feared the jolt against one of those enormous rocks would burst the strips of hide now straining to hold the logs together.

The rocks he glimpsed beneath the water were round, but a crash against one of them, now that their speed had increased, would tear the raft to pieces.

"Perhaps the raft will slow itself when we round the bend yonder," Grandma said. She took her cane, set it across her lap, and held it along with the handle of her satchel in both hands.

"I'll keep working though," Dewey said. "Just in case it don't."

He thrust his oar into the river, and the rushing water rippled around it, creating a wake.

"We're really moving," he said.

"What, boy?" she shouted over the noise of the water.

"Nothing."

"What did you say?"

"I said we're really moving."

"Well, you don't need to tell me that." She looked uneasily at the churning river. Then she said slowly, "I ain't much used to water." The tone of her voice and her expression concerned him and he began to work feverishly to send the raft to the shore.

The river had narrowed. The shore was close on either side, but try as he would, he could not move the raft from the rush of the current. All his paddling was to no avail.

He stopped abruptly, the wet oar against his chest, and looked ahead. There, if anywhere, lay his hope.

Perhaps as they rounded the bend, he thought, a long stretch of lazy water would greet them. Then they would slow and sail smoothly on to Hunter City.

"Are we slowing any, boy?" she asked.

"No'm." He gasped as the raft tipped in the rough current. The water was now white with foam, and it rose and fell like billowing silk, bearing them swiftly to the bluffs.

"Maybe around the bend," his grandma shouted again, as if she hoped to make it true by saying it over and over.

Then neither of them spoke. They waited. Grandma in her chair leaned forward tensely. Dewey gripped his oar. Charlie, on his feet now, whined and shifted unsteadily behind Grandma's chair. They listened intently, without moving.

So it was that they heard the rapids before they saw them. It was a wild noise that filled the air like the drone of a million insects.

"What *is* that, boy?" Grandma shouted.

He did not answer, for both of them knew. Dewey watched wide-eyed as the little raft, unbelievably frail in the tempestuous water, swept around the bend in the river. The water rippled sideways like the flank of a giant horse trying to rid itself of a fly. Then Dewey gasped, and he heard his grandma scream.

There, stretching below them, were the rapids. Through a treacherous crack in the bluffs—it was as if the bluffs had been pulled apart like a ripe fruit— the water ran, dashing against rocks, throwing spray high into the air. It slipped over wide, even boulders, and then turned dangerously green in swirling pools. Then it divided around a boulder as big as a cabin and rushed out of sight.

"Get down, boy," his grandma cried.

He heard her when he was already on his knees, thrown by the force of the first waterfall. He slung one arm about Charlie and then crouched under his grandma's rocker, his other arm anchoring the chair to the raft.

He felt them slip down another fall, sliding easily, and then the raft struck flat on the water, and Dewey's face crashed into the logs with such force that he saw a splash of black. He screamed, tasted blood, then screamed again.

Beneath his arm, Charlie struggled to get free. He braced, tried to pull from Dewey's grasp, using his hind feet to force himself backward.

"*NO*," Dewey screamed. "*NO.*" And he held him by the neck in the crook of his arm. The dog choked, struggled, then was still.

Water washed over Dewey, drenched him, and he looked up just in time to watch them sweep to the left of the huge boulder. He ducked his head and felt the water spray again, cold and powerful as rocks against his back.

They plunged, turned twice, and fell as if they were dropping to the center of the earth. Dewey was in the air for a moment, and then they struck the water, and the rocking chair hit him on the shoulder.

"Grandma," he cried. Water was in his mouth, his eyes, and he thought they had plunged under the water and were lost. He swallowed the icy water and sucked it into his nose as he gasped for breath.

Then, abruptly, it was over. It was like coming out of a nightmare, for they came through the dark shadows of the bluffs into the early morning sunlight. The sun turned the rippling water golden, and then the river widened to fill the broad valley beyond.

Dewey lifted his head. The dog, his fur flattened

over his body, strained to be free. Dewey released him, and Charlie looked around, ready to leap for safety, then found to his surprise that he was safe. The water was smooth now, unhurried, with only the faint sound of the rapids behind to remind them of their recent danger.

"Grandma?" Dewey said.

There was no answer.

"Grandma!" He straightened and raised himself to one knee. "Grandma!"

"I'm still here, boy," she said in a voice that sounded small and distant.

"Are you all right?"

He looked at her. Her clothes were plastered against her thin body. Her hair, always so neatly bound behind her head, now hung in wet wisps. The bonnet she had guarded so carefully hung like a limp rag behind her. But her satchel, wet and flattened over the objects it contained, was still held securely in her lap.

Suddenly Dewey got to his feet. He put one hand up to his eyes to shield them from the sun. "Grandma, Grandma!" He covered her thin shoulder with his hand. "Grandma, yonder's Hunter City!"

Chapter **10**

The Last Stop

He looked for his oar, but it had been swept overboard in the rapids. He thrust his foot over the side of the raft and began pedaling it through the water.

"Grandma, we're at Hunter City," he cried again. "Yonder's Big River. We made it."

"And me looking like a scalded chicken," she said faintly. She moved her hands over her dress, fluttering, straightening the soaked collar, pulling the wet skirt from her legs and squeezing the water from it. "Let's get over there, boy."

"Yes'm."

The raft moved closer to the shore. Dewey could see the white canvas-covered wagons in the clearing. "Help, help, somebody help us," he cried.

Two men appeared on the bank. They looked up, saw the raft with its bedraggled occupants, and stared for a moment in amazement. Then one man ran to the wagons and returned with a length of rope. As the raft approached, he threw one end to Dewey.

The raft was out of the current now and moving

slowly. Dewey stepped around Grandma's chair. He had plenty of time to catch the rope.

"We'll pull you in," one man shouted. "Hold on."

"I've got it," Dewey shouted.

"You men don't go yanking it out of the boy's hands," Grandma said from her chair. She pointed her cane at the two men on shore.

"They won't, Grandma."

"Well, I didn't shoot them rapids to go on no farther. Them men yank the rope too hard, you and me is likely to keep on going to the Pacific."

Dewey braced his foot against one log and then realized that the log was held by only a thread of hide. He stepped back just as the log broke away and moved slowly down the river.

"Hurry, boy," Grandma said. "This thing's going to pieces." With her foot she nudged one of the few remaining logs of the loose flooring.

"I know it."

He pulled the rope arm over arm, and the raft moved into shore.

From the wagon camp came a stream of children, two freckled women with cooking utensils still in their hands, a buxom girl with a baby on her hip, men in dusty, mended clothing. They stood back watching in silence as the raft bumped against the soft, wet earth.

The taller man reached out his hand and Dewey clasped it. The feel of the strong hand filled Dewey with a relief that was deep and complete. Quickly Charlie slipped between them, stepped onto shore, and began to roll over and over in the dry grass.

"You'll have to help my grandma," Dewey said. He continued to hold the man's hand to steady the raft.

"Don't you worry, son, we'll get her off." The other man stepped behind him.

"One moment, young man," Grandma said. She opened the velours satchel, reached into the wet folds, and withdrew the gold-rimmed spectacles.

"Grandma, hurry!"

"This raft ain't gonna last you much longer," the man warned.

Carefully Grandma fastened the slender gold hooks behind her ears. Then she looked up at the man through the watery glass disks. "Now, young man," she said, "you can help me off this here raft."

She stood with difficulty and took the man's hand. Clutching him for support she moved to the edge of the raft, gasped as it dipped into the water, and then stepped onto the shore.

"Ah," she said as she felt the earth firm and good beneath her trembling legs. She was weak, drained of her small strength by the long and difficult trip. "I'll set a minute," she said. She sank to the ground and then straightened. "One of you get my chair," she said, pointing at it with her cane.

"I'll get it." The man lifted the chair and jumped to shore. "Get off, son," he said. "It's breaking up."

Dewey jumped and landed flatly on the bank, leaving perfect imprints of his bare feet in the mud. Then he turned and looked at *The Rosey B.*

Released by the men, it moved slowly down the river. The logs began to spread out like fingers on a hand, and then the last of the hide strips snapped and the logs moved apart.

Behind him Grandma said, "Are the Martins here, would you know? A man and a woman from upriver?"

"The Martins," he said thoughtfully.

Dewey looked up at the man. "They'd be staying with the Sayers," he said. "Mr. Sayers keeps the store." He stopped, then added, "My ma's a real pretty woman who was going to have a baby."

The man paused, scratching the stubble on his chin. "Seem like I did see them folks in town. Two chestnut horses, wasn't it?"

"One was chestnut and the other black—a big black horse, broad." Dewey pressed forward eagerly. "The broadest horse you ever saw."

Behind the glasses Grandma's eyes were sharp. "Speak up, man, did you see them or didn't you?" She waited, her cane held tightly against her, while Dewey closed his eyes. In his mind he could see again the disaster of the Dargan cabin, smell the tang of smoke.

"I think *I* seen them folks," the short man said. "The man was saddling up that black horse just as I was coming out of town. There's Indian trouble and he was right eager to get started home. And the woman—she was all for going right along with him, even though she had a baby no bigger than that."

"Praise the Lord," Grandma said. "They're here and they're all right."

"Yes'm." Dewey was suddenly so weak with relief that he feared he would fall to the ground beside his grandma. His father and mother were safe.

"There's been folks killed and burned out all up and down the valley," the short man continued. "A man rode in this morning with the news. Indians just come down from the hills with no warning—the Weiceks, the Dargans is all dead. Cobuns was burned out. The Lovells got warning and got away, but their place was burned. Them Martins you was asking about was burned out."

"The Martins' cabin was burned?" she asked sharply.

"Yes, ma'am. There ain't a cabin left that I know of."

Grandma looked at Dewey without speaking.

The man continued rapidly, "And it wasn't but seven Indians done it all. They was caught last night, but it won't do them folks no good."

"No. Nobody's done no good by things like this," she said. She sighed. "Fine folks gone, fine places gone." She shook her head and jabbed her cane into the soft earth. "Well, help me up and take me to the Martins."

"You folks part of the Martin family?"

"Yes, this here's the son and I'm the grandma. That man up there saddling his horse is going back up the valley to look for us, I reckon."

"I'll catch him." The short man took the bank in a single leap and ran off through the brush.

Hunter City

"Boy," Grandma said, "I reckon I'll need your help too. I ain't no young girl no more."

Dewey and the man brought Grandma to her feet and then they moved together up the bank. Dewey looked back for a moment, watching what remained of *The Rosey B.* Slowly, lazily the logs drifted around the bend.

"Well, that's the end of it," he said.

"You can make another boat," his grandma replied. "Seem like I heard somebody say one time that wagons and boats just don't grow old out here in the west."

"Mine sure didn't."

"Build it again," she said, "only I tell you one thing. *I* ain't getting on it. I had my last trip on water of any kind. You can build a golden boat with a silver paddle wheel and I still ain't getting on it." She turned to the man. "And you be careful with that rocker, young man. I didn't bring that chair forty miles down the river to have you drop it and break it."

"You folks come forty miles down Trouble River?" the man asked with respect. "You and the boy took the rapids on them logs?"

"We did. My grandson made that raft himself, young man, and a fine craft it was. I didn't think too much of it when I first seen it but it worked out fine."

Dewey felt tears sting his eyes at this unexpected praise. He could not speak.

"Ain't many boys could bring a raft down that river, and that's a fact," the man said. "I know some men that's tried them rapids and been the worse for it. Hey, son, would that be your pa yonder?"

Dewey looked up. Coming toward him with great strides was his pa. Never had he looked taller, never stronger. The sun behind him and the tears in Dewey's eyes made him seem a giant. Dewey began to run and he did not stop until he felt his pa's arms holding him close.

He wanted to blurt out all the hardships of the trip, to tell everything that had happened at once, but all he could say was, "Pa!"

"The boy and the old lady run them rapids on a bunch of logs," the man said. He set Grandma's rocker on the ground. "The old lady never even left her chair." He grinned over Dewey's head.

"Your ma's mighty eager to see you, Dewey," Pa said. He drew back and looked at him. "She ain't gonna believe you're all right till she sets her eyes on you. Come on." He took Grandma by the arm. "Ma, you look chipper as ever."

She turned to look sharply at the man. "You get the chair and mind you be careful with it."

"Ma'am, I wouldn't drop this chair for nothing," he said.

"Your baby sister'll be glad to see you too, I

reckon," his pa said as they started through the brush.

"A sister?"

His pa nodded. "Fine baby girl. Two days old and already bawling louder than a calf."

"And Ma's all right?"

"Fine, son, fine."

"Praise the Lord," Grandma said. "Every one of us is alive."

Behind them Charlie limped quickly up the path. He paused to shake himself. Water sprayed from him in wide arcs and then he continued, brushing past Grandma.

"Don't upset me, you worthless critter. I didn't come no forty miles down the river to have you throw me to the ground."

Charlie moved ahead, content now that he was in the lead, and Dewey paused once again to look at the river. They were on higher ground now, and he hoped to catch one final glimpse of *The Rosey B.* He felt a great reluctance to let her go completely.

"Pa, maybe you can see her from here. She was a strong raft, real strong. I didn't know how to handle her at first because sometimes she went real easy, all by herself like, and then sometimes she would just head where she wanted and nothing I did would stop her."

"Like a woman," the tall man said, laughing.

"Is that some logs over on the other side of the river by them bushes?" Dewey asked.

He stood by his pa for a moment, looking back at the banks, at the shining water, at the brown fading into the green. The man carrying Grandma's rocker upside down on his head paused to look too. Even Grandma turned, one hand rubbing her aching hip.

Abruptly Dewey turned away from them. "No, it's all gone."

"I'm sure it was a fine raft," Pa said, "if it kept you safe." He put his arm around Dewey's shoulder.

The four of them, followed by some of the children from the wagon camp, walked slowly up the rutted road that led into Hunter City. Grandma pulled at her wet, flapping skirt. Dewey looked down at his feet. Pa walked by Dewey, clutching his shoulder tightly and saying nothing. The man with the rocking chair began to whistle.

"First time I been to Hunter City in a year and look at me," Grandma grumbled as they walked into town.

"Neither one of you ever looked any better to me," Pa said.

"Huh! And I ain't got a rag left except what's on my back and what's in this here satchel."

"We'll make out."

One of the boys running behind them stepped up on the other side of Dewey and asked shyly, "What was it you come down the river on?"

"A raft," Dewey answered, still looking at his feet.

"Where'd you get it?"

Dewey glanced at the small boy beside him. "Made it."

"What did you make it out of?"

"I got some logs—nine of them," Dewey said, beginning to warm to the conversation. "Pretty big logs, about like that, and I lashed them together and on top I nailed—"

"Hey, look," Pa interrupted. "Yonder's your ma coming. I told her to stay at the Sayerses', only I guess she had to see for herself you was all right. She's been half out of her mind worrying about you."

Dewey looked up and saw his ma coming toward them with Mrs. Sayers. He could hear Mrs. Sayers saying, "See, look yonder. I told you he was all right. All that worrying for nothing. Look yonder."

His ma said nothing but held out her arms, and he ran to her.

"Ma!"

As she hugged him he was suddenly aware of his muddy clothes and he said, "Ma, my clothes—"

"I was so worried about you, Dewey," she said against his hair. "I was *so* worried."

"Oh, we was all right, Ma, only I'm all muddy and wet and—" He broke off as he heard the squall of the new baby in Mrs. Sayers' arms. "What does the baby look like?" he asked.

"Just like you looked," his ma said.

Proudly Mrs. Sayers lowered her arm, and he saw wrapped in white the small wrinkled face, red as a pumpkin.

He didn't say anything for a moment. He had imagined a plump, golden-haired baby, sturdy and fat, and here was the tiniest thing. He remembered suddenly how disappointed he had felt when his grandma had asked when she first saw his raft, "This here's the boat?" so he said quickly, "I reckon she'll turn out all right."

His ma pushed his hair back from his forehead and then hugged him again.

"Ma, I'm all muddy, I'm—"

"Let's all get back to the house," Mrs. Sayers said firmly. "The boy's tired and hungry and he's done a man's work. And you," she turned to his ma, "you ought to be resting."

And as he started walking toward town, so tired that his knees were beginning to tremble, he suddenly thought that after he had eaten and rested a bit, he would go down to the river and look for his oar. Perhaps it had washed ashore. Jimmy Sayers would help him look, and maybe the little boy from the wagon camp, and if he could find that oar—or even if he didn't find it. . . .

"Someday," he said more to himself than to his ma, "someday I'm going to make me another boat."

Related
Readings

CONTENTS

from **Buffalo Gals: Women of the Old West**

by Brandon Marie Miller

Grandma and Dewey have vivid memories of moving west. This nonfiction excerpt presents the memories of real-life pioneers. These hopeful travelers, many of them women, were not always prepared for the hardships awaiting them.

I have not told you half we suffered. I am not adequate to the task.

—Elizabeth Smith Geer,
the trail's end, 1847

Not long after sunrise on a May day in 1841, a dozen jam-packed covered wagons rumbled out of a small town along the Missouri River. Ox teams pulled the wagons steadily westward toward the Pacific Coast. Most of the 69 men, women, and children in the party walked alongside the wagons. Dawn rose behind their backs, but tonight the sun would set ahead of them, a sign of hope just over the horizon. They were the first trickle in a flood of pioneers, lured by the promise of a better life in the American West.

Difficult times pushed many American families to consider moving west. In 1837 the United States slid into an economic depression. Banks closed their doors; thousands of unemployed workers crowded eastern cities. Farm prices plummeted, and many people lost their land. To make matters worse, diseases like yellow fever, typhoid, and tuberculosis ravaged the country year after year.

For people hit squarely by bad times, the West became a symbol of health, wealth, and freedom. "We had nothing to lose," one woman wrote, "and we might gain a fortune." The journals of fur trappers and explorers, reprinted on the East Coast, told of western adventures. Letters from Oregon missionaries also excited trouble-weary Americans. To many readers, the missionaries' tales of religious zeal paled next to their descriptions of rich farmland, timber, fishing, and furs. Societies sprang up encouraging settlement of Oregon Country. California, too, received good reviews, painted as an earthly paradise of sunshine and lush fruit.

The temptation of cheap land in paradise was hard to resist. During the spring of 1842, another 200 people traveled west. A year later, 1,000 optimistic settlers braved the journey. After the 1848 discovery of gold in California, the numbers exploded to 30,000 in 1849 and 55,000 in 1850. Thousands of European immigrants, mainly from Germany, the British Isles, and Scandinavia, joined the hopefuls heading west.

Most pioneers, especially those heading to the goldfields of California, were single men. But families and some single women undertook the western journey, too. Of the 50,000 people heading west in 1852, about 7,000 were women.

Publishers rushed to print manuals like *The National Wagon Road Guide* and *The Emigrants*

Guide to Oregon and California. Unfortunately, too many guidebooks proved dangerously unreliable. One manual went so far as to assure readers that any notions of toil, hardship, and danger on the trail were products of their "own fruitful imagination." Although women studied the manuals, the books hardly offered a word of advice for female pioneers. How to cook, clean, dress, camp, and care for children on the long adventure was left for women to discover.

Usually, the man of the household was the one who made the decision to pull up stakes and move the family west. While women shared the hope for a better life, many found it painful to sell their homes and sever ties with friends, community, and relatives. Pushing beyond the established boundaries of the United States, early pioneers were emigrants to a foreign, mostly uncharted land. California and the Southwest belonged to Mexico. The United States and Great Britain both claimed Oregon Country, an area so large it included parts of six future states. But few white people lived there. All the western lands were home to Native American families.

A woman's journey west carried an added burden, coming at a time of life when she might be pregnant or caring for young children. The prospect of abandoning society to face months of heat, dust, storms, and "savage" Indians left many women with misgivings. "I have been reading the various guides of the route to California," wrote Losida Frizzell. "They have not improved my ideas of the pleasure of the trip."

Another woman sang a hymn at her wedding only days before leaving for a "jumping off" spot in Missouri. The lyrics asked:

Can I bid you farewell?
Can I leave you,
Far in heathen lands to dwell?

Not all women looked west reluctantly. One new bride, full of youth and enthusiasm, viewed the trip as an adventure with "castles of shining gold" waiting at the end. And Helen Carpenter, a bride of four months, recorded, "Ho—for California—at last we are on the way and with good luck may some day reach the 'promised land.'" Still other women probably shared Luzena Wilson's bittersweet feelings:

> My husband grew enthusiastic and wanted to start immediately, but I would not be left behind. I thought where he could go I could, and where I went I could take my two little toddling babies. I little realized then the task I had undertaken.

Once the decision was made, the journey west could be tackled in several ways. Some people booked passage on a ship and sailed around South America to California. Others traveled to Panama, cut across the isthmus, then sailed up the Pacific coast. By the late 1860s, railroads spanned the continent and provided the quickest, if most expensive, way to travel. Without much baggage but themselves, many single women traveling west chose dusty, bumpy stagecoaches. Stage stops along the route offered crowded rooms and meals of questionable quality. Nearly 3,000 Mormon emigrants embarked upon perhaps the most brutal western journey. Between 1856 and 1860, they walked westward, pulling handcarts all the way from Iowa to Utah.

By far the most popular means of family transportation was the oxen-drawn covered wagon. The typical wagon was built of seasoned hardwood, waterproofed with caulk and tar. Finished, it measured about 4 feet wide and 10 to 12 feet long. The wagon had to be large enough to haul roughly 2,500 pounds of supplies, but not too heavy for eight to twelve oxen to pull. A thick canvas covering was rainproofed with oil. Spare parts—axles, wheels, spokes, and wagon tongues—hung beneath the wagon bed. Other necessities lashed to the wagon sides included water barrels, grease buckets, and heavy rope.

After months of preparation, the wagon sat stuffed with tools, cooking ware, clothes, bedding, sewing supplies, guns and ammunition, a few luxuries, and food. Guidebooks recommended each emigrant carry 200 pounds of flour, 150 pounds of bacon, 10 pounds of coffee, 20 pounds of sugar, and 10 pounds of salt. Added to this were staples of dried beans and fruit, rice, tea, pickles, baking soda, cornmeal, and vinegar.

Buying a wagon and oxen and outfitting the whole project cost between $600 and $1,000. Travelers also needed ready cash to buy supplies along the way, pay ferry costs across rivers, and help set up a new home. Seeking the promised lands of the West was not for the very poor.

ACROSS THE WIDE MISSOURI

Travelers, usually in covered wagons, left their homes in eastern states and perched on the edge of white civilization in Missouri River towns, near the head of the Oregon Trail. More than 350,000 pioneers eventually took this main trail west between 1843 and the late 1860s. At places like Independence and Saint Joseph, Missouri, and Council Bluffs, Iowa, emigrants purchased last-minute supplies, made wagon repairs, and sought advice. Families and solo travelers then joined together in large groups for protection on the trail.

The first leg of the Oregon Trail followed the Platte River toward the Rocky Mountains. Oxen plodded over the plains, slowly climbing to South Pass in Wyoming Territory and the Continental Divide—the boundary between eastward and westward flowing waters. Beyond the Rockies, the trail forked into two routes, one continuing northward along the Snake River in Oregon Country (Idaho, today); the offshoot following the Humboldt River heading toward California.

Emigrants to southern California followed the Santa Fe Trail from Missouri to a split near Santa Fe in New Mexico Territory. The Old Spanish Trail carried on to Los Angeles; the Gila River Trail to San Diego. On any route, travel was slow and often boring, with wagon trains covering only 10 to 20 miles each day. One woman reported that most people in her party had lost track of the day of the week. "Still pressing onward," she wrote. "It is a long and tedious journey."

All along the Oregon Trail, emigrants eagerly kept a lookout for landmarks announcing their progress. In Nebraska, diaries noted sightings of Chimney Rock, towering 500 feet overhead, and Scotts Bluff. Just into Wyoming lay Fort Laramie, followed by Independence Rock, where many pioneers carved their names, and Devil's Gate. Emigrants described antelope and prairie dogs and the excitement of spotting their first herd of buffalo. Most white people had never seen anything like the Great Plains: oceans of tough grass as far as you could see, a huge bowl of sky overhead, and, often, not a tree in sight. Hardly a paradise, the land seemed a fit home only for Indians, the early emigrants thought. Later pioneers, hungry for free land, willingly settled the arid plains stretching from North Dakota down to Texas, and west to parts of Wyoming, Colorado, and Montana.

Guidebooks warned travelers that the journey was "one in which time is every thing." Leaving in spring, when there was grass enough to feed the livestock, settlers raced against the onset of winter more than 2,000 miles to the Pacific Coast. If they delayed for too long, deadly snows might trap them in the mountains that stretched like a wall before Oregon and California.

While the guidebooks reported that the trip would take three or four months, six to eight months of grueling travel was closer to the truth. Days began before sunrise with breakfast, packing up tents and bedding, and hitching the animals to the wagons. After a noon break, travel continued to the next campsite—the best sites provided clean water, grass, and wood. Animals were turned loose inside a circle of wagons, cows milked, tents pitched, supper cooked and cleaned up. After enjoying a visit with fellow travelers and maybe some music around the camp fire, people headed to bed, tired from the day's journey. Throughout the trip, women struggled to keep a semblance of home and family life, but nothing about life on the trail was ordinary.

DONE BRAVE

Cooking was the most necessary daily chore. But cooking over an open camp fire was not the same as cooking on a stove back home, with familiar utensils and a full wood box close at hand. "Although there is not much to cook," lamented Helen Carpenter, "the difficulty and inconvenience in doing it, amounts to a great deal." The first shocking lesson was learning to use the plains' most abundant source of fuel—not wood, but dried buffalo dung. Smoke constantly stung the cook's eyes, and her long skirt soon burned full of holes. Wind and rain made cooking impossible at times, forcing the family into tent or wagon to munch crackers and chew dried beef. Wild berries, fresh meat, and fish were trail treats. "One does like a change," a woman wrote, "and about the only change we have from bread and bacon is to bacon and bread." A sense of humor certainly helped.

Charlotte Pengra's journal entries kept track of her busy trail work:

> April 29, 1853 . . . made griddle cakes, stewed berries and made tea for supper. After that was over made two loaves of bread stewed pan of apples prepared potatoes and meat for breakfast, and mended a pair of pants for William pretty tired . . . May 8 baked this morning and stewed apples this afternoon commenced washing . . . got my white clothes ready to suds . . . I feel very tired and lonely . . . May 14 gathered up the dishes and packed them dirty for the first time since I started . . . May 18 washed a very large washing,

unpacked dried and packed clothing—
made a pair of calico cases for pillows and
cooked two meals—done brave, I think.

Dust coated people, animals, and possessions like a skin. Almost as thick as the dust, and more annoying, were the swarms of fleas, mosquitoes, and gnats. Weather on the journey was unpredictable and often harsh, especially when the travelers' only protection was a tent or wagon cover. "We have had all kinds of weather today," wrote Amelia Stewart Knight, who headed to Oregon in 1853 with her husband and seven children. She continued:

This morning was dry, dusty, and sandy. This afternoon it rained, hailed, and the wind was very high. Have been traveling all the afternoon in mud and water up to our hubs. Broke chains and stuck in the mud several times.

A few weeks later she noted:

Take us all together we are a poor looking set, and all this for Oregon. I am thinking while I write, "Oh, Oregon, you must be a wonderful country." Came 18 miles today.

Wet weather meant wet clothes and bedding, and every so often the baggage had to be hung out to air while the wagon was cleaned and repacked. Heavy chores like this, and the most hated chore—laundry— were usually saved for a special "laying over" day, when travel stopped and work and repairs could be completed.

"THE GOING WAS TERRIBLY ROUGH"

Trail life held dangers as well as discomforts and hard work. People drowned during river crossings; children got lost or fell beneath wagon wheels; buffalo stampedes cost other lives. Disease was the emigrant's constant companion and greatest enemy. The late 1840s and early 1850s saw a worldwide cholera epidemic, and settlers carried the disease west. Victims often died within hours. Smallpox, measles, and typhoid killed others, while dysentery, chills, and fever struck almost every traveler at some point. In June 1852, a woman observed:

> All along the road up the Platte River was a grave yard; most any time of day you could see people burying their dead; some places five or six graves in a row. . . . It was a sad sight; no one can realize it unless they had seen it.

Childbirth in the middle of the wilderness proved another risk. One girl recalled the birth of her baby sister, three days after another sister had died:

> We were so late that the men of the party decided we could not tarry a day, so we had to press on. The going was terribly rough. We were the first party to take the southern cut-off and there was no road. The men walked beside the wagons and tried to ease the wheels down into the rough places, but in spite of this it was a very rough ride for my mother and her new born babe.

Usually sometime in July, wagon trains on the Oregon Trail crossed the Continental Divide at South Pass, a broad, flat plain that disappointed many emigrants expecting something more spectacular. The trip was less than halfway over by this time, and the worst dangers still lay ahead. The California route to Sacramento led through sandy desert, terrible heat, and a climb over the Sierra Nevada range. Oregon pioneers faced the Blue Mountains, the Cascade range, and a trip down the mighty Columbia River before they reached the Willamette Valley.

By this stage of the journey, tension and fatigue weighed on people. Tempers often flared and wagon trains sometimes splintered into smaller groups. "Our company do nothing but jaw all the time," wrote one woman. "I never saw such a cross company before." Taking an uncharted shortcut to save time looked tempting but could prove deadly. All along the trail, furniture and tools lay abandoned to lighten the load for exhausted animals. In the mountains, the struggle grew perilous. Wagons had to be hoisted uphill with chains, ropes, and pulleys, then eased down again with wheel brakes locked.

Oxen dropped dead in their tracks; the road was littered with dead cattle and bones bleached by the sun. "Shame on the man," exclaimed Amelia Stewart Knight,

> who has no pity for the poor, dumb brutes that have to travel and toil month after month on this desolate road. (I could hardly help shedding tears, when we drove round this poor ox who had helped us along thus far and has given us his very last step.)

"WE WOMENFOLK VISITED"

In addition to their jobs as trail homemakers, women helped with men's work, too. They drove wagons, pitched tents, loaded and unloaded, and yoked cattle. If her husband became ill, or if he died along the way, a woman had to manage on her own. One mother, on sheer willpower, got her three children through a ghastly trek in Death Valley. "All agreed," remarked one male traveler, "she was the best man of the party."

Women often relied on other females in their group for help and emotional support. They visited between wagons, spoke of old homes "back in the states," traded ideas to spice up the monotonous diet, and told of hopes for the future. They assisted with childbirth and comforted one another when needed. "Late in the afternoon," said one journal entry, "a group of women stood watching Mrs. Wilson's little babe as it breathed its last." Another woman wrote, "The female portion of our little train are almost discouraged. We sat by moonlight and discussed matters till near 11 o'clock." Exclaimed one woman, "Almira says she wished she was home, and I say ditto!" Women helped each other in other ways, too. On the treeless plains they might stand in a circle, skirts fanned out, providing one another with some privacy during calls of nature.

The months spent on the overland trails were difficult tests. Breathtaking scenery and hope existed alongside discomfort and tragedy. The trails' lessons on adapting and coping with the unexpected helped prepare women for their new lives on the frontier. Some never made it to California or Oregon. But others at last recorded thankfully in their diaries: "This is the journey's end."

from On the Way Home

by Laura Ingalls Wilder

The books Little House on the Prairie, On
the Banks of Plum Creek, *and* Little House
in the Big Woods *are part of Laura Ingalls
Wilder's popular "Little House" series. The
books were based on Wilder's early years
with her family on the frontier, beginning
in the 1880s. Her travels through the West
did not stop there, however. In 1894
Wilder set out by covered wagon with her
husband, Almanzo (called Manly), and her
daughter, Rose, to find a little house of
their own. This entry from her diary
describes one day of their 650-mile
journey from De Smet, South Dakota,
to Mansfield, Missouri.*

July 23

We started at 8. Hated to leave our camping place, it
seems quite like home. We crossed the James River
and in 20 minutes we reached the top of the bluffs on
the other side. We all stopped and looked back at the
scene and I wished for an artist's hand or a poet's
brain or even to be able to tell in good plain prose
how beautiful it was. If I had been the Indians I
would have scalped more white folks before I ever
would have left it.

We could see the river winding down the valley,
the water gleaming through the trees that grow on
the bank. Beyond it the bluffs rose high and bare,
browned and burned, above the lovely green of trees

and grass and the shining water. On this side the bluffs again were gigantic brown waves tumbled and tossed about.

On this side of the James we have passed fields of corn eight feet high. There are cottonwood hedges along the road, the trees ten inches through and 35 or 40 feet tall. But it all seems burned and bare after our camping grounds by the river.

Ten o'clock. It is 101° in the shade in the wagon, and hardly a breath of air.

At 11 o'clock, nine miles from Yankton, we stopped at a windmill to water the horses. The man who owned the house told us he paid $5,000 for three 80's, without a building.

Not far from Yankton we crossed a bone-dry creek bed with the most desolate barren bluffs on each side. Covered with stones and the grass dry and brown, they looked like great drifts of sand that somehow had stopped drifting.

We reached Yankton at 4 o'clock. Drove by the insane asylum. The buildings look nice and they stand in the middle of a large farm of acres and acres of corn and potatoes. Manly wanted to stop and go through the asylum but I could not bear to, so we did not. We passed by the Yankton College, the buildings are very nice.

I am greatly disappointed in Yankton, it is a stick in the mud. We drove all over the town to find a little feed for the teams, went to the mill and the elevator and the feed stores, and finally found a couple of sacks of ground feed but not a bit of flax in the whole town. There were no green vegetables, nor any figs nor dates in the grocery stores. It would be a blessing to Yankton if Carpenter would move down here, or if folks in Yankton would send to De Smet for what they need. They have a number of elevators, 2 or 3 mills, and 6 feed stores, but we carried the most of the feed away in two sacks.

I got my revolver fixed, then we had to spend so much time hunting for feed all over town that Mr. Cooley got to the ferry first. Mrs. Cooley and Paul crossed the river, then the ferry came back and took Mr. Cooley over. It was leaving just as we drove down to the landing at 6 o'clock and while we were waiting for it to come back a bad-looking storm came up. It was not rain, only wind and dust.

We had to face the river to keep the wagon's back to the wind so that it would not be blown over. The wind lifted the hind wheels twice before Manly could get them roped down. The ferryman did not like to try to cross the river in the storm. He waited on the other side until the blow was over, and we were afraid he would not cross again that night. But he did.

Where we crossed the Missouri it is one mile wide, very nasty and muddy. I do not wonder that it is called The Big Muddy, and since I have seen the dust blowing into it I do not think it strange that it is muddy. The Missouri is nothing like as beautiful as the Jim.

Pet made no fuss at all at the ferry, but drove onto it nicely, stood as quiet as could be, and calmly drove off it. Her colt Little Pet ran onto it loose and stood beside her as still as a mouse.

About a mile from the river we camped in woods. Temperature 98°.

Favorite Frontier Songs

The day-to-day struggles of pioneer families took other forms once they reached their destinations. Often they settled in lonely, isolated places. Every member of a family shared the hard work it took to make a section of wilderness into livable farmland. When they could, settlers escaped their hardships by singing or dancing to songs, many of which they learned on the journey west. As you read the words of three songs of the pioneer period, imagine situations in which the Martin family might have sung them.

Oh, Susanna
Words Traditional
Music by Stephen Foster

Paddle Your Own Canoe
Words and Music by Harry Clifton

Buffalo Gals
Words and Music by John Hodges
(also called Cool White)

Oh, Susanna

Words Traditional
Music by Stephen Foster

1. I came from Salem City
With my wash-pan on my knee,
I'm going to California,
The gold dust for to see.
It rained all night the day I left,
The weather it was dry,
The sun so hot I froze to death
Oh, brothers, don't you cry!

Chorus
Oh, Susanna,
Don't you cry for me!
I'm going to California,
With my wash-pan on my knee!

2. I jumped aboard the *'Liza* ship
   And traveled on the sea,
   And every time I thought of home,
   I wished it wasn't me!
   The vessel reared like any horse,
   That had of oats a wealth,
   I found it wouldn't throw me so
   I thought I'd throw myself!

(Chorus)

3. I thought of all the pleasant times
   We've had together here,
   I thought I ought to cry a bit,
   But couldn't find a tear.
   The pilot's bread was in my mouth,
   The gold dust in my eye,
   And though I'm going far away,
   Dear brothers, don't you cry.

(Chorus)

4. I soon shall be in Frisco
   And there I'll look around,
   And when I see the gold lumps there,
   I'll pick them off the ground.
   I'll scrape the mountains clean, my boys,
   I'll drain the rivers dry,
   A pocketful of rocks bring home,
   So brothers, don't you cry!

(Chorus)

Paddle Your Own Canoe

Words and Music by Harry Clifton

Moderately

1. I've trav-eled a-bout a bit in my time, And of trou-bles I've seen a few; _____ But found it bet-ter in ev-'ry clime To pad-dle my own ca-noe. _____ My wants are few,_ I care not at all If my debts are paid when due. _____ I drive a-way strife in the o-cean of life While I pad-dle my own_ ca-noe. _____

Chorus

Then love your neigh - bor as your-self, As the world you go trav-el-ing through, _____ And nev-er sit down, with a tear or a frown, But pad-dle your own ca - noe. _____

1. I've traveled about a bit in my time,
   And of troubles I've seen a few;
   But found it better in ev'ry clime
   To paddle my own canoe.
   My wants are few,
   I care not at all
   If my debts are paid when due.
   I drive away strife in the ocean of life
   While I paddle my own canoe.

Chorus

   Then love your neighbor as yourself,
   As the world you go traveling through,
   And never sit down with a tear or a frown,
   But paddle your own canoe.

2. It's all very well to depend on a friend,
   That is, if you've proved him true,
   But you'll find it better by far in the end
   To paddle your own canoe.
   To "borrow" is dearer by far than to "buy,"
   A maxim tho' old still true;
   You never will sigh if you only will try
   To paddle your own canoe.

(Chorus)

3. If a hurricane rise in the midday skies,
   And the sun is lost to view,
   Move steadily by with a steadfast eye,
   And paddle your own canoe;
   The daisies that grow in the bright green fields
   Are blooming so sweet for you,
   So never sit down, with a tear or a frown,
   But paddle your own canoe.

(Chorus)

Buffalo Gals

Words and Music by John Hodges
(also called Cool White)

Lively

1. As I went lum-b'ring down the street, Down the street, down the street, A love-ly gal I chanced to meet, Oh! She was fair to view.

Chorus

Oh, you Buf-fa-lo gals, will you come out to-night, Will you come out to-night, will you come out to-night, Buf-fa-lo gals, will you come out to-night, To dance by the light of the moon?

1. As I went lumb'ring down the street,
   Down the street, down the street,
   A lovely gal I chanced to meet,
   Oh! She was fair to view.

Chorus

   Oh, you Buffalo gals, will you come out tonight,
   Will you come out tonight, will you
       come out tonight,
   Buffalo gals, will you come out tonight,
   To dance by the light of the moon?

2. I ax'd her if she'd have some talk,
   Have some talk, have some talk,
   Her feet covered up the whole sidewalk
   As she stood close by me.

(Chorus)

3. I'd like to make that gal my wife,
   Gal my wife, gal my wife,
   I would be happy all my life
   If I had her by my side.

(Chorus)

Old Sly Eye

by Russell Gordon Carter

The settlers in this story lived nearly 200 years before the Martin family, but they lived with the same expectation that danger could occur at any moment. Read this story to find out what Alben, a New England boy, might have in common with a prairie boy like Dewey.

It was a May evening in the year 1675. Alone in his father's log house on the northern edge of Dover township in the province of New Hampshire, Alben Hastings lit the lantern and opened his worn copy of *The Pilgrim's Progress*. Suddenly a loud commotion sounded in the direction of the barn—mad squeals and frightened bellowings and the hollow thudding of hoofs. Leaping erect, he seized his musket and, lantern in hand, went racing outside.

He was within a dozen yards of the barn, the wind singing in his ears, when the moon rolled from beneath a formation of ragged clouds, and he checked himself abruptly. There beside the shed lay the recently born calf, and over it crouched a big catlike creature, its solitary eye gleaming, its great round tufted tail weaving savagely to and fro—a panther.

Dropping the lantern, Alben raised the musket and fired, only to see the creature leap sidewise, apparently unhurt. The next instant it swept past him and vanished in the deep shadows.

The boy clenched his teeth. "Old Sly Eye!" he

muttered angrily, and his thoughts went swiftly back to the morning two weeks earlier when his father had set forth with Mr. Stephen Wainright on a prolonged trapping expedition beyond the Piscataqua.

"Yes, my lad," John Hastings had said then, "I know how much you would like to come along, but 'tis your duty to stay behind and look after your mother and sister. And mind ye keep a good watch over the livestock! I wouldn't want to come home and find Old Sly Eye had done to us what he's done to others."

Alben strode to where the calf was lying. It wasn't his fault that Old Sly Eye had somehow managed to break into the barn, for his father himself had said the barn was reasonably secure against varmints. The calf lay motionless—there was no question that it was dead. Within the barn the cow and the two oxen were still stamping about and letting out occasional bellows, but the boy was not so much concerned with them; they were safe and unhurt.

As Alben continued to stare at the calf, he thought of other plunderings within the township—cattle and swine slain by the big one-eyed panther that often killed for the mere sake of killing. Ever since the previous autumn, Old Sly Eye had eluded the bullets and traps of the angry settlers—and tonight he, Alben Hastings, had had an easy shot at close range and had failed to bring the beast down!

Well, regrets wouldn't help. Since the calf was dead, it would serve as food, and therefore the thing for him to do was to hang it on a tree or against the barn, high enough so that nothing could get at it. At the cabin—up in the loft where he and his father were accustomed to sleep—there was a coil of rope he could use. Returning to the lantern, which had gone out, he picked it up and started at a slow walk for the house.

In the south, silver-edged clouds were racing past the moon. He wondered what the hour might be. Perhaps his mother and Rebecca would soon be coming home from the Wainright cabin, a mile or so to the west. They had gone over to help care for old Mrs. Wainright, who had fallen and broken a leg.

The door to the log house was swinging and creaking on its hinges, and as he shouldered his way inside, the wind caught it and thrust it shut behind him. Striding to the fireplace, he groped for the powder horn and bag of shot on the high mantel and reloaded the musket.

On the frontier a loaded musket sometimes meant the difference between life and death. After he had set it down, resting the muzzle against the wall, he crossed the hard-packed earthen floor to the ladder leading to the loft. It would be as black as midnight up there, but there was no need to bother with flint and steel. He knew exactly where the rope was hanging.

With quick, sure steps he started up the ladder, but as his hands closed on the top rung, he felt his heart tighten and his throat go suddenly dry. Something was in the loft—something heavy enough to cause the boards to creak! He was about to back downward when there was a snarl and a rush of padded feet, and the next instant a heavy body thudded against his shoulder and then hurtled past him, knocking the ladder violently sidewise. With a desperate lunge Alben clutched at the edge of the loft, and for several seconds after the ladder had crashed to the floor, he clung there, his legs dangling. Then he succeeded in swinging himself upward.

Old Sly Eye! Crouching on the edge of the high platform, Alben felt the tumultuous pounding of his heart as he stared downward into blackness. The panther was over near the door; he could hear it crooning and snarling. He could hear the occasional thump and swish of its long, heavy tail against the wall. Presently it moved, and he had a partial glimpse of it in a narrow band of moonlight slanting through the opening in the shutter across the south window. He saw its solitary gleaming eye, the other lost perhaps in an encounter with another panther. Then it vanished again in the blackness, and now he could hear it going around and around the room, hissing and muttering, and making other catlike sounds deep within its throat.

Why had Old Sly Eye entered the house? Alben asked himself the question while he was groping about for something with which to defend himself. Was it in hope of finding another victim? Panthers as a rule kept away from humans, yet Old Sly Eye was no ordinary panther. Or was it perhaps curiosity that had prompted the creature to enter the partly open door? The boy could not be sure. He knew only that the panther was down there, unable to get out, and that he himself was in danger.

The loft held no weapon or heavy object that could be used as a weapon. In his two hands he held the rope. It was a stout new half-inch Portsmouth rope, more than a score of feet long—but what good was it? As he finally tossed it aside, he thought longingly of his loaded musket down near the fireplace.

The panther continued to move here and there, now and again passing through the band of moonlight. Every little while it would snarl in a way that made Alben shiver, and once he thought he heard it sharpening its claws on one of the logs. Or was it trying to reach the loft? The logs that formed the walls were unevenly placed—it might come slithering upward. And he was utterly defenseless, lacking even a knife.

Suddenly, with a feeling of icy water cascading down his spine, he remembered his mother and sister. Why had he not thought of them before? They, perhaps more than himself, were the ones who were in danger! Even at that moment they might be approaching the house. They would open the door and then . . .

Perspiration bathed his face and neck and armpits. With cold hands clutching one of the posts, he stared downward, lips drawn tightly across his teeth. What could he do to warn them? Of course, if he should hear them coming he would shout; yet even so, Rebecca might think he was joking. He remembered with regret some of the jokes he had played in the past. But it was possible that they might reach the door before he heard them. The thought of the two of them unsuspectingly entering the cabin sent a chill through him. "I must do something!" he said to himself.

Yes, but what? He was a virtual prisoner in the loft. There were no windows, and the only way to get down was either to jump or slide down the rope secured to a post. In either case the panther would be waiting for him. Again he thought of his musket. Was there any way he could reach it, perhaps with the aid of the rope? No, the weapon was too far away.

The more he pondered, the more he became convinced that the only thing to do would be to go down the rope and then make a rush for the door. It would perhaps take three seconds to go down the rope and another three seconds to reach the door—but during that time Old Sly Eye was not likely to be sitting quietly on his haunches! Alben drew his sleeve across his moist forehead. He was strong and active, but what chance would he have in a barehanded struggle with a powerful panther? Nevertheless, there seemed no other way.

Knotting an end of the rope securely round a post, he gathered up the rest of it, ready to toss it downward. His eyes had by now grown more accustomed to the darkness, and he thought he could make out the panther directly below him. He let the rope drop, and an instant later the house resounded to a frightful scream that set his teeth to chattering. He saw the creature bound like a ghost through the band of moonlight, and then heard it snarling over near the door.

While he waited, listening, he fancied he heard distant voices, as if his mother and sister coming through the forest might be talking to each other—or was it merely the sound of the wind? Raising his own voice, he shouted, "Mother! Rebecca! Keep away, there's a panther in the house!" There was no response. He waited a minute or two and then shouted again. Still there was no response. He had the sudden unhappy feeling that perhaps no one could hear him outside the stout log house—that no matter how much he might shout, it would do no good.

The night was silent now save for occasional gusts of wind and the snarling of the panther and the thumping of its tail against the door. Supposing the door should suddenly open and Rebecca should call, "Alben, are you asleep?" Then the panther would leap and strike—and then . . .

It was more than he could endure! He must risk his life. He mustn't remain idle another moment. But if only he had a weapon of some sort—anything, even a short stick with which he could thrust! Maybe he could find a stick. He would make another search. It would take only a few seconds.

As he was feeling about in the darkness, his hands encountered the blankets that on cold nights he and his father used for sleeping. There they were, neatly folded against the wall. With a quick exclamation he seized one and shook it out. Here was something perhaps better than a stick! The blanket was thick and heavy—at least it would protect his face.

Holding it loosely over his left arm, he seated himself on the edge of the loft, ready to descend. The panther was still over by the door, and he imagined it waiting for him, teeth bared, claws prepared to strike and to rip. Again he thought of the musket. If only he could get his hands on it!

Still holding the blanket loosely over his left arm, he started downward. His feet had hardly touched the floor when a nerve-shattering scream filled the house and a glistening body flashed toward him through the band of moonlight. Crouching, he flung the blanket out protectingly almost at the same instant the snarling panther was upon him.

Perhaps for half a minute it seemed that he and the panther and the blanket were all hopelessly entangled. He could feel the rough wool against his face. He could feel the weight of the creature upon him and smell the strong unpleasant odor of it. Then needlelike claws, caught in the folds of wool, were raking his back and shoulders. Lashing out with hands and feet, Alben tried desperately to free himself. A corner of the blanket covered his head. He reached upward, tore it loose, then rolled sidewise, all the while kicking and struggling.

Suddenly he was free! Rolling twice over, he sprang to his feet. The musket over there by the fireplace! Darting across the room, he snatched it up.

At that moment, above the snarls of the panther still with claws entangled in the blanket, he heard voices outside. It was not the wind; it was not his fancy—the voices were real. With musket raised, he hesitated. Should he risk a shot in the darkness? If he were to miss, it might be fatal, not merely to himself but also to his mother and sister. No, he must not miss! Racing to the door, he flung it wide and leaped outside into the night.

His mother and Rebecca were crossing the clearing from the western edge of the woods. Catching sight of him in the moonlight, the girl shouted, "Alben, what are you doing?"

He paid no heed to her. He was half a score of yards now from the open door of the cabin, musket raised, jaws set. The seconds passed while he waited, listening to the thumping of his heart.

"Alben!" This time it was his mother. "What's wrong?"

At that moment a great tawny, glistening shape appeared in the doorway, its solitary eye gleaming. It swung its head first to the right and then to the left. It raised its voice in a prolonged scream. Then spying the boy, it came bounding forward.

A tongue of flame flashed from the musket, and

the crash sent the echoes flying. They continued to tremble across the moonlit clearing while the panther lay twitching on the grass.

Alben strode to where it was lying. Dead, he said to himself. As dead as the calf! But there were two bullet marks on the panther, one on the throat and the other on the side of the small narrow head, close to one of the rounded ears! Suddenly he understood. His first shot had not missed, after all! Probably it was that first bullet, momentarily bewildering the creature, which had caused it to seek shelter in the house.

"Alben, Alben! Oh, Alben!"

He turned to confront the others. Both were talking to him at once. "Your shirt, 'tis torn to shreds! And you are bleeding! Oh, Alben, are you badly hurt? Tell us what happened!"

He took a deep breath and then smiled. It was easy enough to smile now! "Not so very much happened," he replied slowly. "Yes, I know I'm a bit scratched an' torn, but after all, nobody could expect to fight Old Sly Eye barehanded and not get himself hurt a little!" And then while they gazed at him, wide-eyed, he told them the whole story.

Points of View

by Ishmael Reed

*After their encounter with wolves,
Grandma tells Dewey about how she once
charmed a bear. Discover what the
speaker of this poem thinks about
meeting bears.*

The pioneers and the indians
disagree about a lot of things
for example, the pioneer says that
when you meet a bear in the woods
5   you should yell at him and if that
doesn't work, you should fell him
The indians say that you should
whisper to him softly and call him by
loving nicknames
10   No one's bothered to ask the bear
what he thinks

Song for Smooth Waters

Native American Song

Trouble River begins to live up to its name when Dewey, Grandma and Charlie are tossed and turned by the churning rapids. Then suddenly the water becomes smooth and calm again. These lines reflect the Native American belief in the connection of all things in nature.

Ocean Spirit
calm the waves for me
get close to me, my power
my heart is tired
5   make the sea like milk for me
yeho
yehólo

Granny Squannit and the Bad Young Man

retold by Joseph Bruchac

Even while in danger, Dewey's grandmother demands respect. From the earliest times, Native American elders demanded the same, often telling stories like this one to encourage good behavior in young people.

Long ago, Tooquahmi Squannit lived in a cave near the sand dunes at Cummaquid. Granny Squannit was an old, old woman. She was short and strong, and she wore her long black hair over her face so that only her mouth could be seen. She avoided other people most of the time and knew a great deal about medicine. Even though Granny Squannit lived away from the village at Nauset, she always seemed to know all of the things that were going on with the people. She was especially interested in the children. If a child misbehaved, she might appear suddenly in front of that child to frighten him. It was said that any child who had seen Granny Squannit was always good after that.

In those days, when a boy reached a certain age, it was the custom for him to go through a special initiation to prepare himself to become a man. That boy would be blindfolded and taken out deep into the forest by his uncle to a place where he was expected to stay for three moons. He was given nothing to help take care of himself. While he was gone he would have to build his own shelter and gather his own food. The boy was supposed to think deeply about the responsibility of being a man and caring for the people. This vigil in the forest was not an easy thing to do, but every boy who wished to become a man would do it.

One boy, however, refused to do as his elders suggested. When the time came for him to go alone into the forest, he said no. This boy always thought of himself first and not of others. He would not listen to advice from others. He showed no respect to his elders, even his own grandparents. It seemed as if a bad spirit had gotten into his heart, and there was no way to stop his bad behavior. His father spoke to him, but the boy did not change. His uncle spoke to him, but the boy ignored him. His grandfather spoke to him, but the boy paid no attention. Even the sachem, the old chief of the village, spoke to the boy, but it had no effect. In fact, if that boy was not watched every minute, he would destroy things.

"Where is our son?" his father asked one day.

"I do not know," his mother said, "but I smell something burning."

"Ah-ah! He has made a fire behind the lodge and is burning my arrows!"

The boy was taken to the *pauwau,* the wise old man who was able to cure diseases of the spirit and see deep into the heart of any sickness. The old man looked into the boy's face. He tried his strongest medicines, but they did not touch the badness that held on to the boy's heart. As soon as the *pauwau* turned his back, the boy grabbed the old man's wampum belts and ran down and threw them over the cliff into the ocean.

"There is nothing I can do," the *pauwau* said. "He is a bad young man."

And so that became the boy's name among the people: Bad Young Man. From that time on, no one called him by any other name.

One day, Bad Young Man followed some of the younger children down to the river. As soon as they got there, he began to push them into the water. But as he was doing this, a canoe came up the river. Even though the person in the canoe was not paddling, it cut its way swiftly upstream. And the person in the canoe was Granny Squannit, her long black hair over her face.

The other children climbed up onto the bank and ran, but Bad Young Man stood there in the water, unable to move. Granny Squannit's canoe came right up to him. Then the old woman reached out her arm and yanked him into the canoe. The canoe turned around and went swiftly down the river. Soon it was close to the ocean, near Cummaquid where the sand dunes rose. Granny Squannit pulled her canoe up onto the sand and then yanked Bad Young Man out of the canoe. She held him so hard by the arm that he could not pull away. She took him straight into her cave and sat him down.

Bad Young Man wanted to run away, but he could not move. Granny Squannit came to him with a bowl of green soup in her hand. She gave it to Bad Young Man, and even though he did not want to, he drank it all. And he fell asleep.

When he woke up, four days had passed. He looked around the cave. Where was the old woman who had brought him here? Then he saw Granny Squannit. She was lying across the mouth of the cave and she seemed to be asleep, her long black hair over her face.

If I am very quiet, he thought, I can sneak out and get away from her.

Carefully, quietly, he crawled toward the entrance of the cave. Carefully, quietly, he stepped over the old woman as she slept. But as he was about to leave, he became curious. No one had ever seen Granny Squannit's face. Bad Young Man turned back, leaned over, and pushed the hair away from the old woman's face so he could see what she really looked like. There, staring up at him was—not two eyes, but one! One huge, wide-open eye was there in the center of Granny Squannit's face. It seemed as if that eye were looking straight into the center of his spirit. The boy shouted and fell back against the wall of the cave.

Granny Squannit stood up. She could see that the badness had been frightened out of the boy. She pushed the hair in front of her face and took him by the arm, gently this time, to lead him back into the cave. She took out a deerskin pouch, placed roots and other medicine plants into it, and sewed it shut. Then she gave it to the boy.

"Wear this about your neck," Granny Squannit said. "It will remind you to keep goodness in your heart."

The boy did as she said. He returned to his people and was a bad young man no longer. Before long, he gained a new name. He became known as High Eagle. High Eagle respected his elders and did things with other people in mind. He continued to do good things and gained more respect, until one day High Eagle became Grand Sachem of his people.

Acknowledgments

Continued from page ii

Thacher, Proffitt & Wood on behalf of Ishmael Reed: "Points of View," from *New and Collected Poems* by Ishmael Reed. Reprinted by permission of Ishmael Reed.

BridgeWater Books: "Granny Squannit and the Bad Young Man," from *Flying with the Eagle, Racing the Great Bear: Stories from Native North America,* told by Joseph Bruchac. Text copyright © 1993 by Joseph Bruchac. Illustrations copyright © 1993 by Murv Jacob. By permission of BridgeWater Books, an imprint of Troll Communications.